MW00463315

FORGIVE ME, Father, FOR I HAVE Grinned

V. N. (BUD) PHILLIPS

ILLUSTRATIONS BY
TANNER BLEVINS

The Overmountain Press

JOHNSON CITY, TENNESSEE

ISBN 1-57072-300-1

1 2 3 4 5 6 7 8 9 0

Contents

IN THE CEMETERY

Their Passions Were Strong

The Unusual

UNHOLY LANGUAGE

Acknowledgments

I am truly grateful to all who helped make this book possible. This includes the numerous characters who played roles in the many humorous happenings recorded herein, and those who told the stories to me. I also am grateful to those who helped make this manuscript acceptable to my publisher. And my gratitude knows no bounds to all the kind folks at The Overmountain Press who patiently labored to produce this book and have also played a major role in promoting my career as an author.

Preface

Since the age of fifteen I have traveled all over Dixie and attended church in perhaps more places than I can remember. And I have witnessed and heard about some strange, far-out, humorous happenings in those religious settings that I can never forget. For several years friends have urged me to write and publish these "funny" events. I hesitated for a long time, knowing that in order to tell it like it was, I would have to use some language that is not my common practice nor to my personal liking. But so many of these tales center around the use of unholy language in holy places, that the presentation could not be effective unless I quote certain things as they were said.

It is also true that in some of these tales I have had to give some explicit details in plain language, which some may brand as "ugly." Nevertheless, I had to do it for clarity's sake. Suffice it to say that in all of this, I am merely leading my readers to view and hear a side of life, which, though loathsome to many, is so real that no amount of denial can vanquish it.

Let me further say that I mean no disrespect to any person or church. Much of what is recorded here came to me by the handed-down method. Some I experienced firsthand. A few are "confessions" by actual participants. Many of the people of whom I have written were and are among my best friends, and I have delighted to attend their churches. I accept them with whatever faults or failures they may have, and do not overlook their good works and honorable virtues. I may be a long mile from their faith, doctrines, and practices, but I am at their side in the common effort to create a better mankind.

At least these people, whatever humorous thing they did, helped many to heed the Biblical admonition that laughter doeth good like a medicine. My readers, I have laughed much as I recalled these bits of humor. It is my sincere hope that you may benefit in the same manner.

Bud Phillips
Pleasant Hill
214 Johnson Street
Bristol, Virginia 24201
Telephone (276) 466-6435

$\mathfrak{Holy}$ HUMOR

Humor can be doubly funny when one feels compelled not to laugh, as is usually the case during those infrequent times when rib-tickling incidents occur during a religious service. And of course, in such places, custom and long practice demand that there be no levity. When such incidents do occur, they are usually long remembered by those present, and in many cases the stories are handed down by word of mouth from generation to generation.

Seldom are such things put into writing, but when they are, they often make delightful reading. It should be borne in mind that what is funny to some, might not be to others. Some folks, especially if a bit narrow-minded, may be angered by what others find aisle-rolling humorous.

Certainly, some things happening in a religious setting would not be nearly so laughable if those things occurred elsewhere. But holy humor can happen anywhere, anytime; and the less expected it is, the funnier it usually is. Though these anecdotes cover a broad spectrum of activities, they usually center on unseemly actions at the wrong time and in the wrong place.

MIXED IDENTITY

The Rev. Pickens, an older minister who had been appointed to the Pearson Chapel Circuit of the Methodist Church, near Flowery Branch, Georgia, was definitely of the old school. He still believed in and preached entire bodily sanctification. And like so many of that persuasion, his constant concern was centered in the field of sexual transgressions. Indeed, his first month of sermons consisted of a detailed presentation of the need to observe the seventh commandment. Of course, he had been told that there were some blatant moral transgressors in his church, and that may have inspired his selection of texts.

One bright Sabbath in late August, he had preached long and fervently on the theme that all adulterers and fornicators are certain to provide fuel for the fires of hell. After the service he was invited to the home of Thomas Pearson, whose ancestors had given their name to the local church. Thomas lived a mile or so across the ridges back of the church, where he had a somewhat prosperous farm. He was noted for his success as a cattle raiser, and his pastures were filled with a rather impressive herd.

He had been married twice and had fathered a large family by each wife. The last wife had borne him five daughters, then finally a son, Tommy. Little Tommy never missed a word of the new minister's sermons. He had been impressed by that day's discourse on the sure way to wind up in torment. And, in spite of his tender years, the bright lad had good knowledge of the mechanics of adultery.

The oldest Pearson daughter then at home was a well-developed 17-year-old named Linda. She helped her mother set a bountiful table then quickly went back to the front yard, where her handsome, 19-year-old boyfriend awaited her. The prudish minister had noted, with alarm, the strong courtship between the two youthful people of his congregation. Indeed, he had noticed how the young buck could hardly keep his hands off the girl, even in front of company, and he feared that the boy would probably "ruin" the girl before the summer passed.

Well, it so happened that the Pearsons had a heifer, also named Linda, who up to that day had grazed contentedly in the home pastures. But heifers reach a time when they feel the need to become mothers and provide milk for their owners. That day had come for Linda. Shortly before noon she had become mighty interested in Luke, the herd bull. And not surprisingly, Luke was strongly interested in her.

After the table grace, Mrs. Pearson handed a bucket to Tommy, who was waiting for the second table, and told him to go bring some fresh water. The youngster took the bucket and hurried out past the barn, through the cow pasture, and up the hill to the bubbling spring. On his way back he was shocked at the scene in the pasture behind the barn. The visual image and the sermon connected. Dropping his bucket, he sped toward the house. He must report and stop this mortal sin among the cattle.

Rev. Pickens had just taken an extra-large bite of chicken when the indignant little saint burst through the back door. "Papa, Papa!" he cried out. "Do something quick, or Linda and Luke are sure going to hell. They're out yonder behind the barn, and I saw them commit adultery once, and it looks like they're fixing to do it again!"

The righteous preacher heard the name Linda. And Luke—was that the big buck's name? He couldn't remember. If that was not enough to choke him, what he heard next was.

Old Tom Pearson swung around in his chair and called to a neighbor boy standing at the back door. "Dan, go see if you can't get Luke and Linda through the back gate and into the woods back there, so they can finish up and won't get this boy so excited about what they're doing."

Rev. Pickens hurriedly finished his dinner, excused himself, and quickly rode away. He didn't even take time for some of Mrs. Pearson's fine apple cobbler, which he had already said would be the best course of the meal. Evidently he wanted to spend the afternoon in prayer for his erring young members.

Tom Pearson just couldn't understand why he was not asked to lead in prayer during church services for months after that. And it was nearly a year before the preacher learned that the Pearsons owned a heifer named Linda and a bull named Luke.

Hog Killing Day in Heaven

The rough, hilly, ravine-marked region between Jasper and Pruitt in Newton County, Arkansas, is known locally as "the land between the forks." Sloping upward toward towering Mount Sherman to the west, it narrows to a triangle at the confluence of the Big Buffalo and Little Buffalo rivers to the east. Deep in that area lived "Hog Henry" Harpe.

The home in which Hog Henry lived had started out as a modest, one-room log cabin, but over the years, he had built on to it until it was fairly large. His second wife, Lilly, had an eye for the fancy, so when the last remodeling job was complete, she added lacy Victorian gingerbread work around the porch and under the eaves and gables of the improved and enlarged house. Hog Henry didn't like that so well, sometimes remarking to close friends that it all looked like a barrel of goose feathers in a whirlwind. Of course, he never said that when Lilly was nearby. Like most folks, he expressed his true feelings only to "safe" company.

But like it or not, he spent most of his last days on that porch, where he enjoyed having company come by to sit a spell. The principal road in the locality passed in front of his home, and travelers would often stop a minute to exchange greetings and, perhaps, to inquire of the time. Hog Henry was happy to oblige such a request, but not always in the usual manner.

On his mantel he had an old weight clock that his father had brought from Tennessee about 1855. As Henry grew older, it became a little more difficult for him to arise and go check the time, so he worked out a unique system of telling time so he wouldn't have to get up from his chair.

If it happened to be a sunny day when the query came, he would simply look down at his porch floor and then call back, "Well, it appears that it's two planks and a half till twelve." Or perhaps "It's a plank past three." Or "It's lacking about a half a plank of being four-thirty." All this meant that the shadow on his porch had reached such a designated position. You might perhaps call it his porch dial.

Once in a while, as Henry sat in his rocking chair on that porch, he would tell a friend or interested stranger how he got his peculiar nickname. Indeed, it was not unusual for someone to bring up the subject, hoping to hear again the story of "hog killing day in Heaven." And it was on that porch long ago that I first heard of the odd happenings that led up to his being dubbed with the nickname that stayed with him for the rest of his long life.

On a balmy, sun-bathed day in October, I was warmly welcomed by Hog Henry, who sat in his huge cane-bottomed rocker, puffing peacefully on a corncob pipe. A mutual friend had told me I could get the full story simply by asking him how he received his nickname, so I tried it and it worked.

The gentle, pleasant old man adjusted his horn-rimmed glasses, as if good eyesight might help him think. Looking out toward the surrounding hills bedecked with a grand display of brilliant autumn colors, he began what is doubtless one of the strangest tales of holy humor I have ever encountered:

"When I was pert nigh [almost] growed up, a preaching man come up here from roun' Russellville. His name were Kendall Tidwell, and he started a protracted meetin' in the old Taylor schoolhouse back here a little ways. He stayed at Paw's place, which were nearer the school than I am here. He were a workin' kind of feller and was allus [always] helpin' me with my chores, feedin' hogs and such thangs. Guess that's whar he thunk up his hog idees.

"In no time, that meetin' got to goin' rat pert-like. Folks was a-comin' from fer off to it, some plumb from Jasper and Parthenon. And lots were gettin' religion, some of them powerful strong.

"Lawsy, that preacher could holler so loud, you could have hearn him

— 4 —

fer a mile. And he didn't take the stand nary a time but what he got the glory and jist bucked and stomped around rat lively. You'da thought he was fightin' bees er sumthin! Wish you could've hearn him."

Hog Henry went on to tell how that preacher got on the subject of praying and receiving. Rev. Tidwell became carried away with the subject and finally made the bold claim that if he asked for anything, it would instantly "fall rat slab dab from Heaven." Some in the congregation shook their heads in unbelief, and that became a challenge to the man.

He went a little rash, as some would say, and called out for all to come back the next night and he would demonstrate his faith. "We need meat at our house," he declared," so you all come back tomorrow night and see me pray down frush [fresh] hog meat rat square down from Heaven. It's gonna fall rat here in the middle of this schoolhouse. Just come and see."

As they left the service, many expressed their dismay at the outlandish claims of the "off-brand preacher," as some called him. But dismayed or not, they would be back the next night, bringing many more with them.

The news spread like wildfire. As far away as Parthenon to the south and Marble Falls to the north, folks planned all through the next day to go that night to the old Taylor schoolhouse to see "rail [real] meat fall from Heaven," or at least to see if the off-brand preacher could make good on his promise.

As folks for miles around were talking about the coming miracle meeting, the preacher was "helping the Lord" a little. He had taken young Henry Harpe into his scheme by promising him half of the collection on the coming Saturday night. Henry had figured that his share might amount to two dollars or maybe more, so he gladly consented to help Tidwell help the Lord.

Sometime during that day, Henry slipped a hog out from his farm and took it up a hollow, where he killed and dressed it out. He then transported the fresh meat to the schoolhouse and hid it in the attic, or loft as it was called. Later, he told his mother that he would go sweep the schoolhouse floor and tidy up a bit, because a large crowd of distant visitors was expected. She was proud of her son for being concerned about his religious duties, so she sent him off with her blessing.

"Folks sometimes get hoodwinked now into blessing meanness," Henry interjected at this point in his story, showing his unusual deep insight into human nature. Though young Henry may have swept the floors a bit, his true purpose in going early and remaining at the schoolhouse until meeting time was so he might conceal himself in the attic and wait for time to perform his part in the miracle meeting.

Preacher Tidwell also was anxious to get to the meeting place that night, but he did wait for supper. Though he was expecting heavenly manna, he was still fond of earthly fare! After a hearty meal, he left for the meeting, saying he wanted to go early so he could engage in much prayer before service time. His real intent was to make sure everything was ready for the planned miracle. Back then, even as today, I have noticed, "holy" excuses often were given for deceptive practices.

A small square hole in the schoolhouse ceiling functioned as an opening for the stovepipe in winter. Alas, it also served as an escape route for most of the warmth generated by the heating stove. That hole was to become the passage for the down-coming of the "heavenly manna."

That evening was described by old Hog Henry as "hot as tarment [torment, hell]." The schoolroom sweltered in humid heat, the attic doubly so—so much that he thought "that meat would spile [spoil] before miracle time." In spite of the extreme heat, a packed, standing-room-only crowd filled the little schoolhouse, and many stood outside, peering in the windows and hoping to get a glimpse of manna falling from Heaven. This was expected to be the high experience of a lifetime, and no one wanted to miss it.

There was a sudden pause in Hog Henry's tale when he got to the crowd-gathering part. Looking long out over the meadow in front of his house, he slowly said, "You know, I wonder if Maw missed me from that crowd. Hit's been nigh on to 70 years since that night, and this is the first time I ever thunk of that. Funny, ain't hit, that sich had never crossed my mind. Maybe she thought I was out in the bushes prayin' fer that meetin'. Well, if I was prayin' at all, it was fer the Lord to send a coolin' breeze through the cracks in that hot old loft!"

He quickly resumed the story, saying that finally the service began with a rousing hymn, followed by another and another, rendered with ever-increasing fervor and volume. After hymn time came long prayers. Then Brother Tidwell arose with faith-filled eyes and holy stance, or so it appeared. I suppose any of us could have a strong faith if we knew that the miracle had already been arranged. And then the preacher began. Old Hog Henry seemed to remember every word said:

"Folks, I told you I would prove the power of the Lord Jesus tonight, and I aims to do jist that. Hit's been hog-killin' day in Heaven, I jist know hit has been, fer I feel it deep in my soul. And I know that the good Lord has sent a angel down from Heaven with a load of frush hog meat. And that angel is jist a-waitin', rat in this loft, to deliver the meat to this humble servant."

The mention of an angel so close made some in the crowd a bit nervous, much as if the preacher had said a ghost was waiting to appear. But to others, it only increased their holy expectations.

Then Tidwell walked over to a point just under the square stovepipe hole. Stretching a hand toward the dark hole—which happened to be in the same direction as Heaven—he began his earnest supplication:

"Lord, my sweet Lord, these here folks have come here tonight, some of them from way off, to see proof of your mighty pare [power] and love fer yore humble servant. You well know, Lord, that I need a sight of meat at my house to feed me and my woman and our eight young'uns. Now send me a big ol' fat-jawed hog head."

In the feeble glow of two or three oil lamps and maybe a candle or two, the square hole above was dark as ink. But suddenly there appeared in it a big hog head, which instantly dropped downward. The happy preacher tried to catch it, but it slipped through his hands and flopped onto the floor. Seems that the angel of the Lord was a better pitcher than Preacher Tidwell was a catcher. Now, when that hog head dropped from the hole, the people gasped in surprise and perhaps a bit of fear. One old lady—I think Henry said her name was Sal Wilson—swallowed a load of tobacco or snuff juice, which caused a considerable coughing and spitting fit, but she drew little attention from the beaming preacher and the miracle hole.

Then the preacher, between shouts of joy, called out, "I told you folks, my Lord can do anything. Now you know hit's been hog-killin' day in Heaven, and more meat is gonna fall."

Hog Henry mused that there must have been some in that crowd who thought mid-July was a strange time to kill hogs. Folks around there usually did it in late November or December. "But, maybe," he said, "they allowed that the climate was different in Heaven."

The excited preacher then called up for a nice, big, old, plump, juicy ham. And one immediately dropped down, again missing Tidwell's outstretched hands and landing hard on the floor. Hog Henry told of peering from the hole and seeing Joab Villines, from Erbie, who was sitting near where it fell. Henry watched him draw back suddenly, as if he had just spotted a big rattlesnake, then lean out in the aisle and punch the heavenly ham with his walking stick.

In moments, Joab called to the hushed crowd, "I tell ye, hit's rail meat, folks. I've got my good specs on. And I'm a-tellin' ye rat now that hit's shore rail. Looks lack hit's cornfed too, and jedging [judging] from what hit looks like, I'd say the Lord shore raises a good corn crop and knows how to feed out a bunch of fattenin' hogs." And in spite of the exciting miracle time, he took time to add, "Wonder if they's a good acorn crop up there? Shore not gonna be much of them round here this year."

By that time, Brother Tidwell was really getting into the spirit. Shouting "Glory, glory," he threw back his head and again sought some good meat. "Lord, I shore do like good side meat. Mah Rosey [his wife] can make good use of a big piece to simmer in them good ol' beans. Send me down a big slab of the best you've got."

Instantly, a generous chunk of the requested meat fell to the floor.

Henry laughed a bit when he recalled that, at that point, Walsie Bunch had grabbed her children and dragged them toward the door, hollering out that she was getting out of there, for the Lord was getting too close. He went on to say that he expected lots of folks who claim they would like to see the Lord would run if they did! While Walsie was fleeing, other women had begun to shout, thinking that sweet Heaven was all around them now that a sure miracle was taking place right before their eyes. One of them called out for the Lord to forgive her unbelief. Evidently, she had been sitting in the seat of the skeptical.

As the show went on, Tidwell called for shoulder meat, and it came. He asked for another ham, and it was immediately dropped down by the supposed angel up above. But then the preacher apparently had a little loss of memory; maybe he was too excited to think straight. Throwing back his head and lifting supplicating hands upward, he called out, "Lord, you know my Rosey can make the best souse meat this side of Jericho. And me and them young'uns can eat a dishpan full of hit at one time. So, kind Lord, I need a big ol' fat hog head, so's she can get started soon as I get home."

Alas, there was silence in "Heaven" for a long moment as the "angel" felt around in the dark attic before it suddenly dawned on him that only one hog had been killed and, naturally, it had just one head, which had gone down "the first lick," as Henry stated it. He was hot and tense, and the request for a non-existent hog head irritated him to the point where he hardly realized what he was doing. He suddenly thrust his head through the miracle hole and yelled, "The Lord may grow two-headed hogs, but Paw shore don't!"

Now, if that was not enough shock and surprise to the startled congregation, what happened next was. Henry had stuck his head too far down through the hole, lost his balance, and, in his words, "fell head fomis [foremost] rat plumb down on the schoolhouse floor—jist kersplat rat aside old Joab Villines, who'd been examining the heavenly hog meat." Maybe Joab now thought he had a fallen angel to go with the heavenly meat.

In moments, the crowd knew they had been taken, but not before Tidwell realized that what he had expected to be the grand triumph of his career had suddenly become its greatest tragedy. He tore down the aisle, jumped over Hog Henry (after taking time to grab up a ham), and fled out the front door (he didn't have time for steps, I guess). He hit the ground running and was never seen in Newton County again. The preacher had lost his reputation, but he hadn't lost all the meat. Seems to work that way now both in religion and politics, doesn't it?

Hog Henry ended this bit of holy humor by slowly adding, "Through all that uproar—and that crowd was stirred up like a swarm of bees—I heared my daddy loudly calling out, 'Henry, iffen you ain't plumb killed, I'm gonna limb you good.' Well, I reckon I lost my reputation, too, but I lost a sight more of my hide when Paw got holt of me—rat in front of that crowd, too! But I got something outen that deal that I never lost. That's how I got this quare nickname."

And, having told his tale, Hog Henry Harpe continued to rock in the shade of his "goose-feather" porch.

HE DID SEE SOMETHING

When I lived in southeastern Kentucky, I frequently attended services of the Old Regular or Primitive (Hard-Shell) Baptist churches. Some of the ministers often got carried away during their usually lengthy discourses and might claim to see or hear "holy" things, much to the amazement and thrill of their listeners. This happened one time to Jim B. Collins as he preached during a funeral meeting on Carr's Fork in Perry County, near the gate of a small family cemetery high on a hill above the little town of Vicco.

In the midst of his spirited sermon on the joys of Heaven, Collins threw back his head, placed a hand behind his right ear, and called out, "Oh, sweet Heaven, sweet Heaven. I faintly hear them singing over there. Oh, brethren. Oh, sistern. Don't you hear them? Oh, don't you hear them?" Then he paused, as if listening intently.

A young boy in the crowd piped up and said, "Why, I don't hear anything except them jaybirds a-chirping back there in the bushes!"

But that is not what I started to tell you. One time near Altro in Breathitt County, the Hard-Shells called a funeral meeting for an old brother who had been buried for a year or more on top of one of those sharp ridges so common near Altro.

As usual at such times, several preachers took their turns, with lonesome old hymns sung between each sermon. The first two or three didn't "do much good," as the folks in that area say when preachers fail to get that singsong, low-to-high-and-low-again style—called the holy tone—accompanied by moving and jumping about while jerking their head and wildly swinging their arms in the bee-fighting manner.

Arch Collier arose to take his turn, and the crowd perked up, for he was a sure bet for a long, lively, and holy-toned exhortation. The women got ready to shout, and the men tuned up for a lot of hearty *amens*. Collier did not disappoint. He was soon "fighting" the air, as he swung left and right, bellowing out his spirited sermon, so loud that he could be "heard to the head of Brushy Creek," as one old sister expressed it.

Then the much beloved and respected preacher began seeing things. Looking toward a cherry tree that stood a bit down the hill, he yelled out, "Oh, I see Jesus yonder. Yes, I see my sweet Lord." He repeated the claim several times throughout his preaching.

Well, a nitwit young man in attendance became curious and began looking intently at the cherry tree. Seeing nothing, he then decided to slip around behind the crowd and climb up the tree for a closer look.

Just as the young man got high among the limbs, Collier again peered intently toward the tree and called out his usual claim, "Oh, I see!" And then came a pause, as a half-surprised, half-frightened look swept over his face. "Lordy," he hollered, "I believe I *do* see something!"

That nitwit used to laugh and tell the story, always stating that it was the only time in his life that he was ever mistaken for the Lord.

THE OTHER SIDE OF THE QUESTION

During the early 1800s in eastern Kentucky, ministers were rather scarce. Consequently, when someone died, mourners simply held a burial with no religious rites. Then when a minister happened to pass through the area, he might be asked to conduct a belated funeral service.

And, incidentally, belated marriages were also common. A young couple might simply start living together and then be legally married when a minister became available. This may explain why some of your Kentucky ancestors appear to have been born several years before the marriage date of their parents. At least, I take it to explain why my great-grandmother Cornett was born over two years before any marriage document was recorded for her father and mother.

But getting back to the subject of belated funerals, it perhaps should be told that the custom is still practiced to some extent in the mountain country of eastern Kentucky. Nowadays, however, a funeral is usually conducted at the time of burial, yet years later another service may be held for the deceased. This may seem to be clinging to a now unnecessary custom, but it means much to a great segment of the people who live there.

Small graveyards dot the countryside, often on the slope, or more commonly on the top of a steep hill—and steep hills are not hard to find in the area! Family plots, which sometimes contain a few graves of unrelated persons, are far more common than large, community-type cemeteries.

A burial plot can sometimes be found near—or, on rare occasions, in—the yard of the family home. I know of one woman living near Viper, in Perry County, who buried her husband beside the path leading from the end of the front porch to the nearby outside toilet. She passed by his grave several times a day! It was a clever way of making sure that a family grave was not forgotten.

A small burying ground up Carr's Fork near the town of Vicco is typical of so many in eastern Kentucky. But an incident that happened there in the spring many years ago was not typical of a "standard" belated funeral meeting. On that balmy late May morning, a large crowd had climbed the steep hill to the prepared place of meeting.

The prepared place consisted of heavy, rough boards that had been borrowed from a nearby sawmill and placed on stacks of flat rocks. In front of the improvised benches, a crude stand had been erected. From this the preaching would take place—not that the stand would be much used, because preachers in that area liked the bee-fighting style of delivery.

In the crowd that day were many very old and near feeble folk who had slowly plodded, many with assistance of younger people, up to the little cemetery. Likely, a year later, several of them would be memorialized there or in some similar place in the vicinity. The throng included in-betweens, young folks, courting couples, the ever-present small children, and a smattering of babies in arms.

The few improvised benches could not seat everyone. Many had to stand up back or at the sides. But of whatever description, those present that day waited patiently and expectantly for what they all knew would become a maudlin display of belated grief over the long deceased. They would not be disappointed.

Seven local preachers sat on the bench behind the stand, and all of them would have their say before the service ended. And you could about bet that they all would "drill for water," an expression often used in those hills to describe a preacher who measures his success by the amount of tears he can cause to flow.

The ceremony started with the singing of a mournful, sentimental old hymn, which "Upper" John Cornett would "line out." In eastern Kentucky, many churches do not permit musical instruments in their services, so a liner reads a line of a hymn, the crowd sings it, then he reads another line, and on through the remainder of the song. Upper John (so called because he lived farther up Carr's Fork than did a cousin of the same name) was considered to be the best hymn liner around because he could do it in the quavering "holy tone" so dearly loved by the religious folks of that region.

Following much singing, the preaching started. After two or three had their say, "Little" Irby Hale took the stand. Little Irby, from way up on Irishman Creek, had more zeal than knowledge. Like so many of his fellow ministers, he had a pet peeve. In his case, it was women preachers. And any time he took the stand, listeners were sure to hear a lengthy tirade on the subject. On that particular occasion, Little Irby had great inspiration to speak forth on the matter. For there, sitting on the front bench and looking him straight in the eye, was "Aunt" Mandy Richards, who had been trying to preach for years.

Aunt Mandy, a humpbacked, grandmotherly woman, lived in an old company store building in Scratch Back, which might be described as a suburb of Vicco. Indeed, her home was within a short distance of the cemetery where the memorial meeting was being held. Doubtless she and her husband, "Uncle" Dick, had walked to the place that morning. Though old, Aunt Mandy was, as one of her neighbors so aptly described her, full of fuss and feathers and not the type to "take sass" sitting down.

She was sharp-tongued and often bitterly critical of those whom she had reason to dislike.

Irby had given her every reason to dislike him. They had clashed before. On one occasion she had applied to his denomination (Old Regular Baptist) to be ordained. Of course, she was quickly turned down, and none other than Little Irby had spoken long and loud against her application.

Sitting there that morning, "staring him down," she already had him a bit nervous. Irby, who could "barely talk plain" (as the mountaineers of that area describe those who have speech difficulties), had a strong, pronounced nasal tone that became worse as he "warmed up" in the pulpit. And though he was good at getting the holy tone, his speech impediment all but prevented him from being easily understood.

But Aunt Mandy understood when, with a toss of the head and a swinging of his arms, he "nasal toned" out, "Oh, the womenfolks ist awful bad. There went seven devils outen her."

Then, quick as a wink, Aunt Mandy threw up both arms and loudly called back, "Yes, brother, and there went legions of devils out of the man!"

The wind went out of Little Irby's sails. In moments he yielded the stand to the next preacher in the lineup.

Well, the scriptures speak of mourning being turned into laughter. And that is what happened at the memorial meeting. Up until then, there might have been much weeping among the people, but for several minutes after Aunt Mandy's brilliant rejoinder, there was shaking giggling going on all through the crowd. So much so that the next preacher had a time of restoring the solemnity that was supposed to pervade such memorial services.

Aunt Mandy Richards "passed beyond the veil" not many years after her unusual participation in that ceremony. A few years after her death, Little Irby Hale was laid to rest in the Hale family cemetery on Irishman Creek. Though both are now long gone, their conflict at that memorial service will long be remembered.

Perhaps the next story will explain why Little Irby disliked women preachers.

CANDID CATEY

The doctrine of the Straight Creek Baptist Church didn't permit women preachers or deacons, but the congregation certainly had a woman who "ruled the roost." Old Catey Richards had the final say in everything.

She always entered the little frame church early and took her special high-backed chair directly behind the pulpit. There she sat like a fixed statue through hours-long services, and she made quite a spectacular figure in her floor-length black dress and stovepipe bonnet. From her undisputed throne she peered out at the assembling faithful. When time came for service to begin, it was she who, more or less, determined which of the preaching brothers filled the pulpit. And her choice of songs was usually honored.

Oftentimes there were visiting preachers from the distant hills and hollows of that area (Knott County, Kentucky) in attendance. If "Aunt" Catey approved of these visitors, each was usually given a chance to prove himself. If she didn't approve, then the poor minister or ministers just had to sit silently through long hours of preaching and singing.

One Sunday, "Little" Irby Hale came from over on Irishman Creek in adjoining Perry County to fellowship with the brethren on Straight Creek. He had shortly before confessed a call to preach, and the news had spread over the Knott County hills. Aunt Catey, who had known him since he was a child, consented to allow him to give an exhortation, though she usually was suspicious of beginners.

Irby proudly took the stand, but it soon became apparent that the new preacher was not adept to the old-time, Hard-Shell Baptist style of preaching. Folks there on Straight Creek, like many of their kind all over southeast Kentucky, didn't think one had the anointing unless he had the bee-fighting manner, holding forth in the holy tone. Little Irby just stood still and straight and told his Gospel message in a slow and calm manner.

Aunt Catey became more displeased each passing minute, but she endured it for about fifteen minutes, perhaps thinking he would finally "get the glory." But Irby didn't get it. Aunt Catey leaned forward in a sinister manner. Suddenly she seized him by the tail of his coat and loudly called out, "Fer Gawd's sake, Little Irby, set down and let somebody else get up that can preach!"

FLYING TEETH AT GOBBLER'S KNOB

In memory I can clearly see the Gobbler's Knob church and schoolhouse (the building was used as both). The old one-room, high-ceiling, double-door, frame building, typical of many that served as community centers all over north Arkansas, stood near the head of Piney Creek in Carroll County, just below the knob that gave the community its name. Close by was a large, well-kept cemetery.

Every year in June, folks came to the cemetery from all over Carroll County and from adjoining counties for a decoration service and to enjoy the fellowship and fine food—there was always dinner on the ground—and above all to have their religion stirred up a bit. Of course, the biggest factor in the stir-up was the reminder of loved ones gone on before, and the expectation of being reunited in a better land. As much a homecoming day as a decoration, it was the high event of the year for that community.

After the graves were decorated, largely with homemade paper flowers or home-grown flowers, a big feast was spread under some shade trees. Soon after everyone had eaten to over-full, the main service opened in the schoolhouse, which was filled to overflowing. Many had to stand outside and peer through the windows. No sound system was needed. Those mountain preachers could make themselves heard all over the house and to those standing outside as well.

"Aunt" Mertie Howerton, playing an old-fashioned, parlor-type organ that had been moved in from a nearby home, accompanied the rousing singing for the special service. Watching her pump that organ while shod in high-heeled shoes was rather amusing.

After a few old-time songs, in which virtually everyone present joined, a hill-country preacher would exhort long and loud, frequently referring to the dear departed resting in the nearby cemetery. All this usually had the most emotional of the crowd excited, religiously speaking.

I was staying with friends in the community one year when the annual service took place, and they took me along. And, oh, but weren't those dumplings good—and could I ever forget those fried apple pies? But something else even clearer in memory happened that day.

The family who took me to that high occasion knew to go into the meetinghouse as soon after the meal as possible, in order to get choice seats. We must have gone in real early, for I recall that we sat on the first bench on the right side. I had a good view of Aunt Mertie in her high-heeled shoes as she pumped away on the organ directly in front of us.

The meeting opened with a rousing rendition of "We're Marching to Zion." I have often heard that hymn in years since, but I have never heard it sung with such gusto and sincerity as it was by that assembly of strong-believing hill folk. There were other hymns, including specials by local singing groups. I recall one group sang "How Beautiful Heaven Must Be," and another sang "I Want to Stroll Over Heaven With You." That one really got the tears flowing and put a lot of folks in the pre-shouting mood.

I will never forget the preacher, an old man a bit stooped with years but with a bright, faith-filled countenance. His name was Stanphill, and he was from Green Forest, some 12 or 15 miles away. I have been told that he was an uncle of Ira Stanphill, who wrote "Mansion Over the Hilltop," a song still heard throughout the Southland.

That old-time preacher began in low gear but soon made it to overdrive as he waxed eloquent on his theme, "This world is not our home; we are just passing through." After about 45 minutes of good hard preaching, he then got the holy tone and began to walk back and forth across the stage, hands on his back and patting his foot to the tune of his preaching.

On the front left pew sat Lawson Self from way down on Dry Fork. "Uncle Laws" was a tall, gangling sort of fellow, long faced with a matching nose. A great mop of unruly near gray hair crowned his head. As the sermon picked up steam, he leaned forward, chewing, as if savoring every word. His face grew redder by the minute. I later learned that all these signs indicated that he was about to "get the glory."

About that time Brother Stanphill launched into the last statements of his sermon: "Well, I'm a pilgrim and a stranger here. Sweet Heaven is my home. I can be at home anywhere down here, be it a cottage or a mansion. Yes, anywhere is home sweet home. Now, folks, let's all join in and sing 'Anywhere Is Home.' And while we are doing it, let's have a good old-fashioned handshake and love feast."

Aunt Mertie, who had remained on her organ stool all through the long sermon, pulled out all the stops, pumped away, and roared out with the familiar tune, as the crowd joined in with amazing volume. Then the handshaking and hugging began.

The singing and love feast had barely started when Uncle Laws got the glory. Yelling like he was in a fox chase, he ran back and forth, here and there, shaking hands all the while. He got on the stage and darted back and forth, still shouting to high heaven. The crowd outside began to close in around the windows, eager to see and hear the excitement going on inside.

Finally Uncle Laws spotted Clyde Howerton, a devout but quiet Christian, peering in through the left side window at the end of the stage. Very fond of Clyde, Uncle Laws made a lunge for him, reached out, and took his hand. "Praise the Lord, Clyde, ain't the Lord good!" he yelled, throwing back his head. "I'm a-thinking about your dear grandmother that I growed up with over here on Osage. She was a real saint if there ever was one. But she's done outstripped us and gone on ahead. This world was not her home, and it ain't ours either. Oh, we're going to see her on that great resurrection morning."

Inside, Aunt Mertie continued to pump the organ and slam at the keys, as the crowd raised the roof singing and shouting. An old sister near the stage heard Uncle Laws's exhortation and squalled out like a wildcat with its tail in a trap. Two or three others joined in her religious spell.

That did it. Uncle Laws, still holding Clyde by the hand, threw back his head once more and ripped the air with a yell that could have been heard clear to Osage. But, alas, the old fellow wore false teeth. That tremendous burst of air dislodged them and shot them out the window, hitting Clyde square in the face. Well, the shouting saint had mind enough to call out, "Catch them, Clyde. I'll be out and get them when this spell wears off."

And with no teeth, he shouted on.

How Preacher Green Lost His Toupee

Shortly after I left home at the age of 15, I wandered into the mountains of eastern Newton County, Arkansas. High on the steep northern slope of one of the most picturesque of these mountains stood the old Addison schoolhouse, surrounded by endless stretches of uninhabited forests. Yet anytime preaching services were announced for that location, those woods became alive with numerous mountaineers and valley dwellers, all swarming toward the rustic board-and-batten building. Many of them walked or rode horses from distant communities.

It seemed that everyone in the area enjoyed "meetin' time" at Addison, especially when the widely known and well-loved Josh Green was the speaker. The fiery old backwoods preacher had conducted some memorable services there, including one that, I dare say, no one present ever forgot. That's when he lost his toupee—and more!

Rev. Green had been slick bald-headed for longer than most of his neighbors could remember, and he probably would have gone on that way had he not begun wooing the young widow Payne. But something about his courtship with the 29-year-old made him want to wipe away evidence of his 60-plus years, and look youthful again.

A younger half brother, who lived at Harrison in adjoining Boone County, told him that there was a place in Springfield, Missouri, that sold what he called false hair for baldheads. The thought of having his head covered with hair again thrilled the love-sick preacher to the point that he sold a fine plow mule in order to have money for the purchase of the coveted hairpiece. Soon afterward he rode with a local cow buyer to that southern Missouri city, where he walked from the stockyards over into the business district and made the purchase.

The Springfield barber, while perhaps a good salesman, apparently was not too adept in the art of cosmetic restoration, for he sold his aging client a thick, wavy, jet black toupee. It might have done something for a 25-year-old, and it did something for someone of 62 years—but not in a positive manner!

However, Rev. Green was proud of his new hair. Riding back through the Ozark hills, he kept running his fingers through it and occasionally leaned over to see himself in the rear-view mirror of his neighbor's truck. Somewhere along the way, he remarked that his plow mule (referring to the cost) "shore" looked good on his head.

The widow Payne, pleased with her suitor's new hair, gently told him that now all he needed to finish the job was a set of false teeth. He had been smooth mouthed and sunk jawed for years, but to please his sweetheart, he allowed he would go into Jasper and see if his old friend, Dr. Binam Moore, would make him a set on credit.

Dr. Moore obliged, and soon Rev. Green was trying to eat with something other than his long-hardened gums. While in Jasper, he stopped at Rufus Arbaugh's drugstore and picked out a pair of "ready made" eyeglasses. He wasn't sure they really helped him see better, but he secretly thought they might add a bit of dignity and refinement to his appearance.

He had seldom ever worn anything finer than new blue overalls, even when filling his preaching appointments. But at Jasper he learned of a rummage store above the post office. He ventured upstairs to see what might be available in the way of dress clothes. The store had one suit that fit him, but it was solid white. He plunked down his last dollar for it, thinking of how his fair lady would delight to see him in something other than his usual humble attire. The kind woman who operated the Save the Children Federation Store came through with the gift of a well-used white shirt and a nearly new black bow tie to go with it.

Soon after becoming restored, he sent out word that he would preach at Addison the following Saturday night and twice on Sunday. By dark on Saturday, the small schoolhouse was packed to capacity, with many standing up in back and some outside peering through the open windows. And it was rightly thought that many in the crowd had come just to see the newly renovated preacher.

When he finally entered the door with the widow Payne at his side, everyone saw that there had indeed been a change in Rev. Green. He tried to walk erect (he was a bit stooped), but his too strong glasses caused him to stagger and step high. His heavy black hair, with its many waves and curls, glistened in the light of a half dozen oil lamps. The teeth had so filled his shrunken mouth that his face had a distinct pear shape. And the black bow tie appeared to be a continuation of his hair, as it stood out sharply against the vast background of white shirt and suit. Of course, his many-time-wire-repaired plow shoes looked a bit out of place with his grand dress, but few could see them in the shadowy schoolhouse. He was quite a contrast to the humpbacked, sunk jawed, baldheaded, overall-clad preacher to which his congregation had been long accustomed.

When sermon time came, he mounted the stage with what appeared to be new zeal and energy. Insects swarmed around the oil lamps in the summer night. But he didn't seem to mind the heat or the occasional bug that might perchance fly into his ear or mouth. He just dug out the ear, or spat the bug from his mouth, and preached on, sweeping his arms in the "bee fighting" manner of delivery. Back and forth he sprang across the stage and swung time and again around the crude pulpit, clapping his hands and occasionally pounding the walls to drive home an important point.

To his right was what the local folk called the spitting door. It remained open, even in cold weather, if certain tobacco-chewing preachers came for a service, for some of them had to often pass near it to unload their profuse tobacco juice. And, of course, it was open that hot night.

While jumping about near that door, the greatly excited preacher gave his head a quick snap. Whatever secured the toupee to his head suddenly gave way, and the valued hairpiece went sailing off his head and fell to the floor. But Rev. Green was so up in the spirit that he didn't notice. And in that moment, as the crowd sat stunned, he swung around and, for some reason, looked downward. Through his too-strong glasses he saw a dark, furry object near his feet.

"Great walls of Jericho," he bellowed out. "Iffen they ain't some sort of varmint done creeped in here." He gave the "varmint" a great swinging kick toward and through the open door. Wouldn't you just know that an old hound dog standing outside the door grabbed the flying mass of fur and began slinging it left and right.

The widow Payne screeched out, "Lordy, Josh, that weren't no varmint, that were yore hair!"

Rev. Green stood stunned for a moment then slapped the top of his head. Realizing the excited woman was correct, he quickly lunged through the door at the growling animal. But the hound dog sprang across the narrow clearing and into the bushes, still slinging and shaking the hairy mass.

"Come here, fellers," the preacher called back inside. "Help me run this infernal hound dog down. He's done got my plow mule in his mouth!" And with that he bounded into the dark brush, yelling as he went, "Come on, fellers, let's run the old sinner down."

When he finally gave up and returned to the schoolhouse, the ruin of his restoration job was complete. Neither dog nor hair could be found. His teeth had been lost somewhere in the dark bushes because of his wide-mouthed yelling. A low limb had knocked his glasses from his face. Somewhere out there, his black bow tie had dropped from his collar. And his white suit, now splotched from numerous encounters with dew-wet leaves, was covered with a great deal of yellow mud from frequent falls in the dense brush.

But restored or not, the widow Payne became his bride before the summer ended. She bore him a large second family and tenderly cared for him until he died at the age of 92. As long as he lived, he would always say that he'd "rather have a good plow mule any day, as a wad of false hair that wouldn't stay put no how!"

When I Played the Hypocrite

Pretending to have a religious experience is one common definition of hypocrisy generally accepted in church circles. If that definition is correct—and I think it is—then I, author of this book, am clearly guilty of once playing the hypocrite, and in a very pronounced manner!

It happened in Lawrence County, Tennessee, in a little farm community in the hills west of Shoal Creek and not far from Lawrenceburg, the county seat. Though two or three denominations were represented there, the strongest by far was the Pentecostal church. In the early 1950s, this group met in an old, but well-kept, former schoolhouse. Two or three times per year, they held long-running revivals.

The event of which I tell happened during the spring revival. It was the liveliest of the year, perhaps because the members had been kept in a bit during the winter and were anxious for the "holy exercises" certain to be a part of the services. The evangelist at the time was Stephen D. Wilkins from near Florence, Alabama. A Pentecostal of the first order, he always created a noted stir wherever he went.

I was staying in the home of a Mr. and Mrs. Young, who were among the most enthusiastic of the Pentecostal believers in that area. Of course, I went nightly with them to the big revival. The service became more interesting (and that's putting it mildly) night after night. Near the end of the first week—first week of four, that is—Mrs. Young decided she would like for an aunt of hers to come stay with her through the remainder of the meeting.

The aunt, Lucinda Hayes, lived just across the line in adjoining Giles County. A dyed-in-the-wool Pentecostal, she was a stronger believer than the Young family, if that was possible. At the least, she was more prone to proclaim and demonstrate her faith. Mrs. Young knew that her super-religious aunt would enjoy the meetings and perhaps add a great deal to them. She was right on both counts!

Lucinda (called Aunt Cindy by the Youngs), a big, puffy, old lady, possessed a bitter/sweet personality. She could be sweet one minute and then easily switch over to the bitter side. No matter the mood, she tended to be overtalkative, expressing opinions without regard to the consequences.

She also had the unholy habit (as folks in the area put it) of calling the Youngs—including the children, ranging in years from about six to sixteen—to prayer at about five o'clock each morning, even if all had been kept at the schoolhouse until midnight and likely not in bed till an hour later.

The late revival schedule was just about a nightly occurrence. So every morning I would be awakened from a deep sleep by loud supplications going up in the living room, which happened to be next to the bedroom where I slept. And the family, once up, stayed up. Breakfast was served about six.

As I am not an early-morning person, such a schedule was not to my liking, but I conformed as cheerfully as I could. I suppose I have done lots of conforming in my time that wasn't by choice but was of seeming necessity. But don't we all do that?

Aunt Cindy also insisted on a prayer time before the family went to bed, even though they had been where praying was done numerous times during the evening revival service. I pondered on why God had to be reminded of their needs so often, and in such a loud manner. Whatever the need, they sure kept the wires open to the great communications center above!

Aunt Cindy and her niece always took a midafternoon nap, as did I. They shared a bed, an arrangement Mrs. Young had made as soon as her aunt came. (I found out later that she did this so there would be no "unholy thoughts or actions" between the couple while a revival effort was going on. I couldn't help but wonder how her husband felt about it.) Both women were overweight, and I am sure the double bed wasn't quite double enough.

One afternoon about three o'clock, they retired to their bedroom, on the opposite side of the house from the room where I slept. I went to bed at the same time. I was almost asleep when all of a sudden I heard a commotion in the room where the ladies were napping. It startled me because the first thing I heard was Aunt Cindy shrieking to her niece, "Lord God a'mighty, don't you see him, Nancy, don't you see him? He's rat over there in that dark corner by the closet door."

Her exclamation was quickly followed by the creaking of the rusty old bedsprings as the pair jumped up. I froze in fear, wondering if some man had slipped into the house and hidden in the closet and was then coming out to attack the women.

Then there was a shout from Aunt Cindy, followed by her screeching, "Hit's him, hit's him. Don't you see him, Nancy?" Apparently, Nancy wasn't seeing, for then the aunt excitedly called out, "He's a-comin' rat towardge us. Rat there he is." In a lower and puzzled tone of voice, she quickly added, "Well, where did he go?"

I soon learned, much to my relief, Aunt Cindy had awakened and seen a vision. She vowed it was none other than Jesus Christ and he had appeared in the bedroom and then faded away before Nancy could see him. As things settled down again, I heard the old aunt earnestly asking Nancy if there could be sins in her life that caused her not to see the holy image; however, I could not hear the answer.

But this is not what I started out to tell you. It was just a memory that surfaced as I recalled that time so long ago. What I really want to tell you happened during supper on Monday night of the second week of the by-then rip-roaring revival. Nancy Young set a delicious supper that night, with turkey and dressing for the main dish. Maybe that stirred certain reminiscences with Aunt Cindy.

Eagerly devouring the food on her plate—as was I—the super-religious old woman reared back a bit and, out of the blue, called out, "Law, ain't the power of God wonderful? I trust in the Lord for everythang, even thangs that would seem powerful foolish to people who don't believe much."

"Oh, glory, yes," Nancy replied. "I'm a-trusting my sweet Jesus for everything, little or big, and I'm doing it more and more every day."

"Oh, praise the good Lord," Aunt Cindy went on. "I'm so glad to hear it. Land, I recollect way back durin' the depression, I was raisin' me some turkeys so that I could sell them and make a little money, which I needed plumb bad. You know, them turkeys lived an' done well rat up to about time to sell 'em. I was real hoped up about gettin' that extra money. And bless God if they didn't get a plague among them, and started dyin' off a sight. Now there was no time to get any medicine. Of course, I don't believe in medicine, no how. So, praise Jesus, I took my old black-backed Bible and went out rat amongst them and read that promise about no plague comin' nigh my dwellin'. Then I raised my hands and started prayin' fer them turkeys to be healed. I knowed that if God saw the fall of every sparrow of the air, he shore could see a big old gobbler a-floppin' down and dyin'."

By then I'd felt the giggles welling up within me. I yet am easily tickled and may have been more so in those youthful days. I could always vividly imagine things, and the picture of that woman out among the turkeys, reading the Bible to them and praying for their healing, struck me as funny. I wondered how I might make a quick and graceful exit but could think of none. For I well knew that the story was going to become even more comical.

Nancy threw her hands up and cried out, "Oh, glory, glory, I jist know the sweet Lord helped you out."

"Oh, land, yes," Aunt Cindy called out, as she tossed back her head and rolled her eyes. "Dear God in Heaven, I never seed sich a time. All of a sudden, the power from Heaven struck me rat in top of my head, and hit struck ever' blessed one of them sick turkeys at the same time. I jist fell under the power. And even though I was a-layin' down, I went to dancin' in the spirit, jist lack a body would do iffen hornets got under the cover with ye."

An image instantly flared in my mind. First I could see that big, puffy, old woman lying flat on the ground among the turkeys. That was hilarious enough. But when she spoke about that dance like "when hornets got under the cover," I could clearly visualize such a thing. What could I do?

I was bursting inside with suppressed laughter—you know the feeling. It was one of those times when I would've given a thousand dollars just to have a wild, near hysterical laughing fit. But during that "torture," I remembered something.

The Pentecostals in that area had a belief and practice that I have found in only one other group of that faith. They believed in, and sometimes practiced, what they called the holy laugh. Sometimes during their meetings, a brother or sister would "get in the spirit," and instead of talking in tongues (as many such groups do), the person would be seized with seemingly uncontrolled outbursts of laughter.

By that time, Aunt Cindy was leaning back in her chair, stomping the floor, and waving her hands. The thought flashed through my already overloaded brain of how funny it would be if she leaned a little too far and fell back in the floor. Well, that notion about raised the pressure to the exploding point. And Aunt Cindy continued on:

"Glory! Glory! Nancy, them turkeys jist began jumpin' up and down. I bet they was jumpin' knee-high above the ground, and when they'd hit the ground, they'd jist dance circles and kick, and some of them got down a-rollin' and a-gobblin' rail fast lack. Oh, the good Holy Ghost had hit them, shore."

Now Nancy, doubtless envisioning a Pentecostal meeting where folks might behave in the same manner—she knew that at such times there was usually a lot of talking in unknown tongues, to show that the power had truly come down—began swinging her arms, stomping her feet like dancing while seated, and cried out, "Great holy Jesus, Aunt Cindy, did them turkeys gobble in the unknown gobble?"

That did it! There was only one thing to do. I couldn't jump up and run, knowing that if did, I'd be laughing to high heaven before I could get out of hearing. So I suddenly stiffened, threw up both hands, and cried out, "Oh, hallelujah, glory to God, praise sweet Jesus." Then I burst forth with what had to be the most spectacular and loudest demonstration of the holy (as unholy as it was) laughter that ever struck in Lawrence County or anywhere else. Once in a while I could catch my breath enough to shout, "Oh hallelujah, glory to God, thank you, sweet Jesus." Then the shrieks of belly-shaking laughter would break forth again.

Old Cindy jumped up, turning over her plate and water glass in the process, but she didn't seem to notice. She danced and shouted around the table, yelling, "He's got hit! He's got hit, glory to God, he's got hit."

As tickled as I was, I recall breathing a prayer of gratitude that my ruse had worked. Nancy just fell backward in the floor and began that "layin' down dance" so recently described by Aunt Cindy. And that didn't ease my laughter any. I laughed and hollered on, and Aunt Cindy danced, shouted, and talked in the unknown tongue.

As usual there was a long testimony meeting in the revival that night. Old Aunt Cindy could hardly wait to get up and tell how Brother Phillips had been struck with the laughing power at the supper table. "And, oh, hit were powerful strong," she said. "Hit stayed on him fer a good five minutes or more." Then she added what was likely a true statement: "I tell ye, in all my years of servin' the good Lord, I ain't never seed such a strong spell of the holy laughter."

It may have been the greatest display of laughter she ever saw, but it sure wasn't holy!

The Wrong Door

A lot can happen when a wrong door is used, figuratively or literally. The door of which I write caused a great deal of excitement—excitement that most of us would find humorous—but to the actual participants, it was a disaster.

Many years ago a traveling preacher (some old-timers called him a circuit rider) stopped for the night at a humble home about a mile above Hayter's Gap, on the North Fork of the Holston River in Washington County, Virginia. He was on his way to Chatham Hill, but a dark, rainy night had overtaken him, and he needed shelter.

He was kindly received, and the hostess served a plain but ample supper that included a large pan of yellow-meal corn bread, which the preacher dearly loved. Needless to say, he partook heavily, washing it down with thick buttermilk and cold spring water. Before he finished eating, another traveler arrived. He too was served supper, and he had in common with the preacher a great love of yellow-meal corn bread.

After dinner, the hostess cleared the table. Both travelers noted with much satisfaction that she placed the remaining food in a huge cupboard with a floor-length door that sat beside the back door of the house. The men harbored hopes that she would serve the leftover corn bread with sweet milk for breakfast, as was commonly done in the area.

As the evening passed, it became apparent that the second traveler was far from being a preacher. Clearly hostile, embittered, and hedonistic, he told some stories that wouldn't exactly be welcome in a Sunday school class. But the host family and the preacher patiently endured him until bedtime. When the old-fashioned clock on the mantel struck eight (a common bedtime in the country at that time), the two guests were shown to a bed in a little room at the end of the kitchen.

Some might say that the lion and lamb had lain down together. But bed sharing by traveling strangers, no matter how different, was also common. The situation often led to hostile activities, such as when one of the sleepers became a cover hog and rolled up in all available blankets and quilts, leaving his bed partner shivering in the cold. No such problem developed that warm night. But something else did!

The dark, moonless night was made for sound sleeping. Fog had begun to form in the nearby hollows and coves in the shadow of the towering Clinch Mountain. The only sound was a soft but steady rain falling upon the low roof over the room where the travelers slept. Both were soon snoring, perhaps dreaming of corn bread and milk.

About the time that the clock on the living room mantel struck two, the "unholy" traveler was awakened by a need to do something about the buttermilk and spring water he'd tanked up on at supper. He groped through the kitchen and finally found the back door. As was often done in the hills at that time, he went no farther, but just stood in the open door and "let fly."

On the way back through the kitchen, he doubled up a toe on a table leg. The pain resulted in a jumping, foot-swinging fit during which he lowly released a torrent of some rather wicked words—at least, they sounded so to the preacher, who had been awakened by his bedfellow's journey and accident. But for the sake of peace, he said nothing. Snoring soon filled the little bedroom again.

About an hour or so later, the preacher also felt a need to "go stand in the door." He went to the kitchen, groped about until he found a door handle, opened, and let fly. When he returned to the bed, his bed partner awoke and promptly inquired of the conditions outside, likely thinking of long miles of travel on the coming day and concerned about weather conditions.

The preacher replied, "I can hear rain still hitting on the roof, it's dark outside as a barrel of black tomcats, and for the world, everything smells like corn bread."

Just as he was stretching out, pulling up the cover, and thinking he might have two more hours of sound sleep, his bedfellow suddenly stiffened, raised up, and looked down at him in the dark. With both fear and anger in his voice, he inquired, "Which one of them doors did you open—the first or the second?"

"Why, I just opened the first door I come to. Weren't that the back door? As I remember, there was just one door back there."

"Hell and damnation no," the furious man bellowed out. "The first door is the cupboard, and I bet you shore done it rat in that big pan of corn bread. I jist know you did. Why, you damned, stupid, old fool! You done now ruined our breakfast, and that woman [the hostess] is gonna be bilin [boiling] mad. I'm gonna kick you out of this bed and beat the hell out of you."

He began to fight but got the surprise of his life. The meek and mild preacher fought back like an enraged bulldog. Around the floor the men scuffled, going at it claw, tooth, and nail. The preacher uttered not a word, but the other combatant cussed with every breath.

Over the little room they rolled, and when near the outer wall, their wild kicking sounded like someone trying to tear down the house. Somehow in the melee, the covers were dragged from the bed and kicked about over a rather dirty floor. That was not going to please the hostess.

Suddenly a candle flared in the living room beyond the kitchen, and there were excited voices of folks rousing out of a deep sleep. After all, it is disconcerting to be awakened by the sound of a pitched battle going on only a few feet away.

By that time the unholy traveler had the preacher backed up against a wall, banging his head on it. "Damn you, you blundering fool," he angrily called out. "I'm gonna knock some sense into your fool head."

But the glowing candle and the booming voice of the approaching host brought a sudden end to the hostilities. "What in tarnation is going on in there?"

Both men knew that the jig was up and they'd better flee as quickly as possible. They separated and grabbed what clothes they could find in the darkened room. Not pausing to dress, they dashed into the dark, rainy night, mounted their horses, and fled, the preacher riding swiftly up toward Chatham Hill, the other man going down the North Fork.

Doubtless, the household was puzzled as to what had happened. After all, neither guest had paused to offer an explanation. Perhaps the mystery was solved when the lady of the house brought out the pan of corn bread and found it a bit soggy and giving off an unusual odor. Indeed, it was several years before the story of the wrong opened door got back to the host.

UNHOLY THOUGHTS CANCEL BAPTISM

To understand this tale, you need to be familiar with a regional term. In most parts of our country, the word *courting* simply means dating or, as some folks would say, going together. But in the mountains of southeastern Kentucky, the word once had, and to some extent yet has, a far deeper implication. It indicated that a male and female were seeing one another and much, much more. Our modern teenagers would call it "going all the way." Even now, it pays to be careful in that area and not say, "So-and-so are courting"—unless you are prepared to prove it.

Near Ulvah, in Letcher County, Kentucky, a long creek known as Line Fork has its confluence with the North Fork of the Kentucky River. The creek got its name because it was the dividing line between the lands of my great-great-grandfather William Cornett and his brother Samuel.

Far up this creek once lived "Uncle" Jonah Collins, a man of pioneer stock—which means much in that part of the country. He owned a nice spread of land and was considered better off financially than most folks in the vicinity. Highly respected and looked up to by his neighbors, he had been a hard worker all his life and continued strenuous activities into his advanced years.

At the age of 75 (the time of this story), he still entered into his farming and blacksmithing activities with the gusto of someone half his age. And local rumor was that he also entered into certain other activities with the interest and energy usually conceded to the younger bucks of the community.

Uncle Jonah had attended a nearby Old Regular Baptist church all his life, but he had never tried to live in it (an expression in that region that means to become a member). He had strongly supported the church with money and work, and even assigned himself a special job there.

In summertime, services were held with the door standing wide open. Dogs who had followed their masters to the meeting place often "decided for a little closer fellowship" and would walk right into the building and perhaps lie down in the aisle. There had been times, at some slight provocation, the dogs had barked and sort of destroyed the solemnity of a service in progress. No preacher, and likely not many in the congregation, wanted the coarse, loud barking of an old hound dog mixed in with the preaching of the Word.

So Uncle Jonah cut a long walking staff (longer than he was tall) and kept it handy as he sat near the front door. If a dog tried to wander in, the animal received a whack over the head from that walking staff wielded by the guardian of the door. That itself caused a little disturbance, especially if the hurt dog barked and snapped out its displeasure, but it was considered less than if loud barking had been in the church.

There came a time when Uncle Jonah's wife, Sarah Combs Collins (known as Aunt Sis), got religion, "powerful strong" as the neighbors expressed it. She had, according to her telling of her travels to the church (describing her conversion), gone to a bean patch to pick a mess for supper. While there she began thinking on the ways of grace; she surrendered, and the assurance of pardoned sin flooded her soul. According to her testimony, and confirmed by Uncle Jonah, she got so full of glory that she tore around the bean patch, shouting for joy, and became so carried away, she didn't realize she was destroying lots of the vines in the process. "Jist tore up that bean patch" was how Uncle Jonah phrased it.

In accordance with the teachings of her church, Aunt Sis desired to be baptized, and she sent for a beloved cousin of hers to do it. Rev. Hiram Combs lived way down the Kentucky River at a place named Jeff. Well-known throughout the mountains as a kingpin preacher of the Old Regular Baptist faith, he often traveled to distant points to preach or baptize. According to the testimony of others, he had the knack of turning a simple baptismal service into what some of the better educated called a spectacle that would never be forgotten. Maybe Aunt Sis wanted her baptizing to be something her neighbors would long remember. In any case, when she called on cousin Hiram, he favorably responded.

Just across the bottom field in front of Aunt Sis and Uncle Jonah's home was a water hole of Line Fork Creek, a beautiful and suitable place for the baptism. A large crowd of relatives and friends gathered at the Collins home on a Sunday for a feast of delectable country grub before assembling on the banks of Line Fork for the sacred service. Rev. Combs was prominent among the crowd as he gathered choice food for his plate. Having done so, he retired to the front porch and took a seat by Uncle Jonah for a time of fellowship while the two devoured Aunt Sis's unbeatable chicken and dumplings, along with other good food.

The two had known each other for over 50 years. They had become acquainted when serving in the Civil War and, over the long years since, had maintained a pleasant friendship. Anytime Rev. Combs preached in that area, even though miles of mountains and hollows might have to be traversed to get to the place, Jonah always went to hear him. But the good minister had never been able to pull his old friend "over the line," as he called it. But sitting there that day, and on that special occasion, Rev. Combs thought that perhaps an opportune time had come to persuade Jonah to surrender and cast his lot with the people of God.

"Well, Jonah," the white-bearded and white-haired (what hair he had left) mountain preacher slowly began, "me and you are old men and not long for this world." He had no way of knowing at the time, of course, that they both would live over 20 more years. "And whatever we are going to do, its about time we did it."

Uncle Jonah quickly agreed, and Rev. Combs continued, "Now, I made my peace with the Lord might nigh 50 years ago. It was just after I returned from the war, and I got baptized right off by old Long Dave Maggard, down there at the mouth of Carr's Fork. And glory to God, I'll never forget it, for it marked my beginning of a life that has been filled with joy and peace ever since. I know I'm going to sweet Heaven someday. And I want all my friends and relations to meet me there, where we can have blessed fellowship forevermore. Now, Jonah, don't you think it's high time that you got right and got baptized, like dear old cousin Sis is about to do? Why, I could do it right here today—put you both under at this meeting."

Uncle Jonah looked long across the field toward where the baptism was supposed to take place, then he slowly replied, "Yes, Hiram, I've been thinking a sight here lately about doing right and being baptized. Fact, I got to thinking of it yesterday when I was plowing down yonder in the old Tid Watts field. And just as I was thinking the strongest about it, here come down the road that strip of a gal of Simpson Lyle's, and it's well-known around here that she'll heist [hoist] her dress and back up against a tree for anything that's got britches on. And you know when she got nigh the Watts field, just a twisting and shaking her middle parts as she went prissing along that road, my mind got strong on courting, and I plumb forgot all about doing right and being baptized. And in spite of myself, I've had courting on my mind ever since!"

I venture to say that Jonah was probably more honest than many who sit in the amen corner today.

NOTE: I once boarded in the home of a couple who lived near where this incident took place. Indeed, the man of the household had been present and heard Uncle Jonah make his honest confession. His wife, a first cousin of my mother's, more than once confided to me that she thought her 80-year-old husband was still having extramarital affairs. One day, as all three of us sat on their shady side porch, the husband again told the story of why Uncle Jonah couldn't think of being baptized, ending with a hearty laugh. But during that tale and laughter, his wife was looking spears at him. Then, when all was quiet, and with hard ice in her voice, she spoke: "Yes, there's too many old men around here now who's studying about courting."

SPECIAL CASE

One long, hot summer many years ago, a young, healing evangelist had come to Bristol, Tennessee, and was trying hard to make a great impression on those of the particular brand of religion he espoused. He had stretched a huge tent in a large lot just beyond East Hill Cemetery and down a side street to the left of East State Street. He drew large crowds with his nightly displays of what he called miracles. A local funeral home had agreed to haul in bedfast cases, and this in itself created special interest. (Alas, when no miracle occurred, those cases had to be taken back to their homes).

One sultry night, the healing line was especially long. Still, the compassionate preacher took time to ask each seeker what his or her trouble was. A huge Amazon of a woman, a well-known prostitute of the city, finally reached him.

"What seems to ail your body?" he asked. "But remember, the good Lord is able to cure all diseases."

"Well," the old gal began, "I's got backaches, headaches, heart trouble, my kidneys are bad, sight of rheumatiz, awful high blood pressure, can't hardly see, and the doctor says I am starting on diabetes." She paused, trying to think of other ailments, then added, "I reckon it's a sight what all is wrong with me. I guess just tell the good Lord that I's just like an old worn-out car needin' an overhaul job."

And behold, if that preacher didn't lay hands on her and call out, "Lord, it looks like this dear old woman is about plumb worn out. Now, good Lord, get hold of her and overhaul her good, from the engine to the running gears and plumb out to the tailpiece!"

I was there and heard the entire thing.

Hot Prayer and Cold Dumplings

Not long after I moved to the Bristol area, I found employment in the welfare department of the local Salvation Army. Naturally, I felt obligated to attend the religious services of that organization, and I soon became friends with the Army's quartermaster, George Sutphin, and his lovable wife, Maggie. They were delightful people, and both were refreshingly eccentric to a marked degree.

It was evident that they had endured much hardship in former years. George was born in the woods (as he expressed it) near Roan Mountain in Carter County, Tennessee. He had never been too successful in finding gainful employment. Maggie was raised near Bristol and had early married a much older man. She bore him two children who both died very young, followed closely by the elderly husband. Somewhere along the way, she met George, and they soon were married.

Living near Bristol and almost destitute, they came to the attention of the local Salvation Army commander. He brought them into town to work for him and secured living quarters for them on an upper floor of the King Building in the first block of Fifth Street. George became the manager and cook for the Salvation Army Transient Lodge. Maggie assisted in the transient work and did other tasks for the local commander.

At that time the Salvation Army was headquartered in a former residence at 20 Fourth Street. The transient lodge was housed in the former carriage house (later garage) and servant quarters in back of the main building. George cooked a huge pot of beef stew every day, and the delectable smell would waft all over the block. Soon folks began calling him "Beef Stew" Sutphin, a handle he never totally lost.

By the time I arrived in Bristol, the Sutphins were uniformed soldiers of the local corps, and George had volunteered as quartermaster. The Army no longer employed them at that time, for George had found a job as a janitor with the S. E. Massengill Company and had rented an apartment in the old Parson Burroughs house at 117 Third Street.

George was a slow walker—he just crept along—but he was quick witted. One time, an agnostic who worked at the Massengill plant asked him how he knew that there was a devil. In a flash, George told the man to go to a nearby restroom, where there was a full-length mirror. "Just look in that mirror," he said, "and you will meet the devil face to face!"

A few weeks after I met the Sutphins, they invited me to their home for Sunday dinner, and I gladly accepted. (They always called the noon meal dinner, as have all my family and acquaintances for as long as I can remember.)

The invitation was repeated time and again in the months that followed. On that first visit, while Maggie prepared a pot of chicken and dumplings—one of my lifelong favorite dishes—George entertained me in the living room by playing a few of his more than 900 old 78-rpm records. The aroma that drifted in from the kitchen stirred my appetite as the music delighted my ears. Finally Maggie called us to dinner.

Once seated at the table, we bowed our heads while George offered thanks for the meal. I think he wanted to impress me with a long and well-said prayer; he prayed on and on, mentioning needs that were far outside of table grace. The hot bread cooled, and the steam from the dumpling bowl fell lower and lower.

Maggie was growing impatient. Whenever she was displeased, she would hiss, something like an angry goose. She would even do this in church if things did not suit her. Well, she started hissing at the table that day. But George paid no heed. As he droned on, Maggie began a low muttering. "Lord God, George," she began, "for goodness' sake, bring it to a close." After another strong hiss or two, she muttered, even louder, " Lord God, George, the stuff's gettin' cold. Whew, when on earth are you gonna stop? I'm a-starvin'." Then, referring to me, she added, "And I think this young'un is too."

As she hissed and muttered on, George went down the list of former corps officers, asking special blessings upon each one. He prayed for Captain so-and-so and Lieutenant such-and-such. Finally he came to a place of fervent intercession for the beloved Captain Carr, who had served the Bristol Corps many years before.

Maggie hissed loudly and exclaimed, "Land sakes, George, he ain't no Captain now, he's done been promoted to Major!"

George flushed red, and his ever-present nervous tremor became a little more pronounced, but he prayed on: "You know now, Lord, whether he's a Captain or Major. This durn fool woman can't hardly read a blessed word, and I know you can read the *War Cry* a sight better than she can!" (The Salvation Army's magazine always carried a list of officer promotions.)

With that, some rather hot words erupted between the two, ending the table grace. Indeed, the pair had hot words, but a little later, when tempers and the food had cooled, we had to be contented with cold dumplings.

Bluff Bob Gamble

Long before I knew how he got his strange nickname, I knew Bob Gamble. When I first met him, he lived in the rugged country near Harrison, Arkansas, where he and younger members of his family operated a fruit stand at the side of State Highway 7.

Actually, he had little to do with the operation of the stand. He spent most of his days sitting in an old cane-bottomed chair near the end of the fruit-display porch. There he constantly chewed his tobacco cud, never seeming to mind the overflow of juices that sometimes dripped from his chin. He delighted to talk to anyone who would stand or sit a spell within hearing of him. He can best be described as kind and gentle, a lover of people, and one who gloried in being able to tell someone something, usually in a humorous vein. His humor often contained bits of golden philosophy and sound advice.

His wife, who also spent most of the summer days sitting on the porch—they both moved inside and sat by a large, potbellied stove in winter—was just the opposite. I doubt that I ever heard her say a dozen words. But she always seemed to be listening.

Both were very religious. In fact, Bluff Bob had long been a deacon in a nearby Baptist church. He often spoke of his strong faith. Again and again he would mention how he always trusted the Lord for everything, and when he was in trouble, he immediately called for divine help. He would go on to tell of times of marvelous deliverance.

But there had been one occasion when it looked like it was too late for even the Lord to help, and that is when he got his nickname. I didn't hear the story from him, however, because he never talked about it. I had to find out from his nephew who was with him when it happened.

Erbie, Arkansas, where Bob had formerly lived, is on the Big Buffalo River, which I consider to be one of the country's most unique and beautiful waterways. Designated America's first national river in 1972, the pure, free-flowing stream has not been significantly altered by industry or man. Along its course through Newton County are numerous sheer limestone cliffs, some of which tower more than 200 feet above the lucid waters of the winding river. Often at the tops of these cliffs are sloping earthen banks covered with small, loose rock, making it extremely hazardous for anyone to venture too close to the edge. As one old-timer expressed it: "Ye can git a good view of the valley from the top of them bluffs, but iffen ye ain't careful, you'll soon be down at the view." Well said.

Bob liked to squirrel hunt along the high ridges above the Buffalo valley. One day he took his teenage nephew, his trusty rifle, and the family dog on a hunt not far above Erbie. The dog soon picked up the trail of a squirrel and went yelping and tearing through the low brush that covered the side of the ridge. Bob took after them, gun ready and looking intently down at the ground in front of the rushing dog.

Shortly the chase led to a fallen tree. The racing squirrel and pursuing dog passed under the tree, but Bob could not. He whirled to the left in an effort to go around the obstruction. Still watching the dog, he did not realize he was heading downhill toward the edge of a cliff. Before he knew what was happening, he was on the earthen bank, and the loose rocks were rolling him swiftly toward the edge. There was no bush to grab.

His nephew, running not far behind, realized the danger and managed to put on the brakes in time. As he did so, he heard his uncle bellow out, "Lord help!" just as Bob slid over the cliff and plummeted downward. Then the teenager heard a plaintive yell from farther down: "Ah, hit's too late now!"

It was not such a high cliff, and the water down below was deep. A good dunking in Buffalo was the worst that happened to Bob. Alas, his trusty and highly treasured rifle sank into the water, never to be found again. Though he'd lost a fine rifle, he gained a nickname.

The nephew told of the incident, and news soon spread for miles around. From then on, he was known as Bluff Bob Gamble.

CRAZY JIM FELKINS GETS A "HEELING"

During the first month I lived in Tarrant County, Texas, I attended church in a little community not far from Fort Worth. It was a friendly country church led by an aggressive and capable young pastor whose name I no longer remember.

But I have not forgotten how he patiently endured an unusual situation in that church. It certainly appeared that he had submitted to the Biblical precept stating that charity suffers long and is kind. At least his tolerance kept the church operating in peace and love.

Attendance was healthy, with visitors at nearly every service. But not all the visitors appeared to be holy or there for a holy reason. Indeed, I think the man who directed me to the church, rather than having an interest in promoting increasing attendance, wanted me to have the "shock treatment" he knew would come.

As I took a seat near the back, a large family came in. Among them was a man who just didn't look right to me. I took him to be a mental defective, and I would soon learn the accuracy of my instant diagnosis.

The enjoyable song service was what I expected in a country church of its type. After announcements, a prayer, and a special song, the young minister called the ushers forward to receive the offering.

Just as the ushers took their place before the minister, the strange appearing man leaped up, hit on all fours, and scampered down the aisle. Suddenly he stopped, turned his nose up, and called out, "Oink, oink, oink, I'm a hog, I'm a hog." He then ran a little farther, stopped again, put his nose down toward the floor, and yelled loudly, "Bow-wow, bow-wow, I'm a big bad dog, and I'll bite the first one that tries to stop me." He then whirled and went bucking and snorting toward the pulpit, calling out, "I'm a horse, I'm a wild horse."

He next lay down flat and, in a twisting motion, crawled along the aisle. This time he announced he was a big bad rattlesnake, ready to strike at any leg that got in his way. Then he jumped up and headed back toward his seat, shouting that he was a wild man gone slapdab crazy and he was going to run loose through the woods day and night. When he reached his seat, he sat down and remained quiet and meek through the rest of the service.

I was shocked—as most everyone would be if someone in church suddenly started such unexpected antics. I was further shocked by the fact that no one in the congregation, except another visitor or two, paid any attention to him. Most folks were busy digging into wallets and purses in anticipation of the upcoming morning offering. The minister stood silent, as did the waiting ushers. I had expected a commotion when the man leaped into the aisle, but there was not the least semblance of such. The unusual display seemed as acceptable as any part of the Sunday ritual.

Before the next Sunday came around, my friend who had sent me to that church explained. The man was known as "Crazy" Jim Felkins. The church was full of his relatives: brothers and sisters, nieces and nephews, uncles and aunts, and even an aged grandmother. All the relatives were fond of this demented member of their clan, and they resisted all efforts anyone dared make to correct him. In fact, two or three former ministers who had tried to do something about it had quickly been made to seek another church, as involuntary as their actions might have been. The non-Felkins group, which was small compared to the ruling family, had just accepted the situation and meekly bore it. And the new pastor had conformed.

Every Sunday at the same point in the service, Crazy Jim put on his "little show," as my friend described it. "Show" it was—one I never forgot!

I should have attended one more week. As it was, I found a church to my liking in Fort Worth, much nearer to where I lived. The next Sunday after I left that church in the country, Crazy Jim's antics took on a new twist, and the congregation did pay attention to him. If attention is what he craved—and the more discerning of the group had long said that was the cause of his childish doings—he got it, perhaps in a larger measure than expected.

Occasionally, travelers passing by on the busy highway picked the church as a place to worship before journeying on, which probably was the case with a woman who showed up that Sunday. The service had already started, so no one had a chance to find out who she was.

She appeared to be tired and somewhat nervous. Like so many drop-in visitors, she took an aisle seat near the back. As usual there were three or four other visitors, those who did not look so pious, present that day. (Talk of the strange part of an otherwise conventional service had spread far, and rare was the service that a few did not appear just to see the happenings.)

Offering time came, and Crazy Jim began his ritual. The lady traveler jumped and gasped when he started. She tried to scoot over away from the aisle, but others in the full pew blocked her. By the time Crazy Jim got even with where she sat, he was into his dog act. He fixed his eyes on the terrified woman and loudly *bow-wowed*, stretching toward her as if ready to attack.

Well, she attacked first. She swung a leg out at him in an attempt to kick. He took advantage of her move to sink his teeth into the calf of her leg. The woman screamed, jumped around though still seated, gave another shrill scream or two, and then kicked again like a striking rattlesnake. Her high-heeled slipper crashed like a hammer into his left temple.

He yowled one time and rolled across the aisle and stilled against the opposite pew. He was out cold. The panicked woman hopped up and in two or three wild leaps was out the front door and racing to her car. She "dug a wheel," and the gravels flew as she left the parking lot before roaring down the highway at a terrific speed.

By then the congregation was on its feet and in an excited uproar. One old lady, who couldn't see what was happening, yelled to another who was in the aisle and asked what was going on. The lady in the aisle yelled back that she thought Crazy Jim had "gone crazier" and was attacking people.

He might have been crazier, but he didn't act like it from then on. Perhaps the lick in the head had a beneficial effect. He never again put on his animal act, in church, or elsewhere.

AUNT HET'S EVERLASTING FALSE TEETH

"Aunt" Het's dentist had told her that her new false teeth (seldom called dentures in Brantley County, Georgia, where she lived) would outlast her. Indeed they did, but not in the way expected.

Aunt Hettie "Het" Cadle was long a faithful member of the old Pine Flat Baptist Church. She was, in fact, a very conspicuous member. And not so much by her active participation in church services—though she was ever-present when anything went on at Pine Flat Baptist—but she stood out in that congregation because of her enormous size.

At six feet, two inches tall, she was above average height for a woman, and the remainder of her body was plenty large to match. Not that she was all fat—far from it. Actually she was quite muscular, and those muscles had a good chance at being well-developed, for she was her husband's best sawmill hand.

Old "Mill Bob" Cadle operated the largest sawmill in Brantley County. Aunt Het, his best off-bearer, caught the huge slabs from his log squaring and carried them away to a nearby pile. That's a strong man's work anywhere, especially during the south Georgia heat. And there had been occasions when she used her well-conditioned muscles for other purposes. Over the years, more than one sawmill hand had become contrary with her, to the point she felt compelled to settle things with more than her tongue.

Her attire also caused her to stand out in a crowd. She had an everlasting propensity to wear bold-patterned Sunday dresses often with life-size or larger flower designs, sometimes with blue or red birds hovering about them. She made her own dresses in the plainest form (though brightly colored) with straight lines from top to bottom, as one would make a large sack. Her high-topped, buttoned Sunday shoes were of the fashion 50 years earlier. She always carried her purse wrapped in a salt sack, upon which the lettering was still clearly visible. She topped her ensemble with a broadbrim hat to shade her light-sensitive eyes, and when she walked or talked, the artificial roses around the crown bobbed about like ships tossed on a stormy sea.

Aunt Het was considered Brantley County's best chicken-and-dumplings maker. Whenever there were occasions for dinner on the ground at the Pine Flat Baptist Church, she brought a half-bushel pail full of her delectable specialty. Some folks knew that she used the same pail to carry excess chicken manure from her little pine-pole henhouse to her garden and flower beds, but the love of her unsurpassed dumplings usually overcame what qualms one might have had concerning her multipurpose pail.

Chicken and dumplings became a much preferred meat dish in her home, both by her because of ill-fitting false teeth, and by her totally toothless husband. (After he saw Het's bad experience with her dentures, he would not even consider paying out hard-earned sawmill money to buy himself a set.)

And that brings us back to Aunt Het's teeth. Her dentist may have given her assurance of long-lasting quality, but he apparently made no promise that they would fit. To call those teeth ill-fitting is putting it rather mildly. When she talked—which was nearly all the time—her teeth danced about in her mouth with a resulting *clack-clack* sound that was a bit disconcerting to pleasant conversation.

The clacking was especially noticeable when she took her seat in Pine Flat Church and began lively conversation with those seated around her. The old gal just couldn't be near anyone without much talking, and she usually did the talking for her listener, as well; that is, she gave no time for reply. Knowing that her clacking teeth bothered others, she developed the habit of removing and holding them dripping in hand, as she rambled on.

But when it came time for the service, she would slip them back into her mouth, which occasionally was a sad mistake. For, you see, Aunt Het sometimes had prolonged shouting spells. And the first wild whoop usually dislodged those teeth and sent them zipping through the air, sometimes with disastrous results.

One time they shot into the back of Myrtle Stout's bare neck. Myrtle always pulled her hair up and pinned it on top of her head. She was half asleep, but the unexpected and sudden encounter with Aunt Het's teeth awoke her, at least partly. She must have been dreaming that a vicious dog was pursuing her, for she sprang up and lunged forward, screaming that she was "dog bit" right in the back of her neck. It didn't help matters any when her sister, sitting near her, yelled out, "Hit's not a dog, Myrtle, hit's Aunt Het."

Myrtle, terrorized at the thought of Aunt Het suddenly going crazy and attacking her, lunged left, toward the long part of a well-filled bench. She then lunged to the right, where only two people separated her from the aisle. She jumped over them and tore out of the church, screaming as she went. All the commotion created a considerable stir in the church. Some of the folks, especially the young "sinners" of the congregation, shook and giggled through the remainder of the service.

Anytime Aunt Het shouted her teeth out, there was an interruption of the service. No one would pick them up, thus making it necessary for the toothless woman to hunt them. And when she found them, she made quite a show of straightening up and trying to fit them back into her mouth. She was about half blind and would sometimes try to place the uppers where the lowers belonged.

Needless to say, some in the congregation made fun of the poor woman. Among the most blatant was "Flirting" Marge Kimmons and her third husband, Lucas "Luke" Simerly. (Folks had quit trying to keep up with her married names and just referred to her by the name she had carried from birth.) The two young folks—Marge was only 19, and her husband was a year younger and still pretty much a kid at heart—did little to suppress their giggles. They often mocked her, going through the motions of removing or inserting teeth while Aunt Het did the real thing. She sometimes frowned at them but made no real fuss about the matter.

Another thing that most of her friends found amusing was the fact that she always removed her teeth before eating. She seemed to want them less when you would think she needed them most. Even at a public dinner she would take them out in plain sight of everyone, often licking the teeth a bit and then wiping them dry on her apron before depositing them in her pocket.

Once, Aunt Het worked all day bearing off slabs at her husband's sawmill. After coming home, she hoed out her cabbage patch and then weeded a flower bed before cooking a five-course supper, including chicken and dumplings, which she and Mill Bob ate ravenously. After the dishes were washed and put away, the couple sat on the kitchen porch for some much desired rest.

The evening was hot and humid. Sundown doesn't bring much relief in that part of southern Georgia, so the two sat long, fanning vigorously, he with an old magazine cover, she with a large paper plate. Suddenly she looked intently at her husband and made a strange and certainly prophetic statement: "I think there will be a big gathering at Pine Flat before Sunday is here again."

Those were her last words. Her head fell forward, her teeth fell into her lap, and with a long sigh, she was gone.

Indeed there was a big gathering at Pine Flat Baptist Church before Sunday arrived again. Folks came from near and far; friends and relatives from Waycross and Folkston showed up to hear the last words said over the legendary Het Cadle. And there, in the Pine Flat Cemetery, old Aunt Het, ill-fitting teeth and all, was laid to rest under the red Georgia clay.

Next Sunday there was a distinct spirit of quiet sadness in Pine Flat Baptist Church. However, the meeting soon became rather lively, in an unusual and unexpected way.

After a mournful hymn, well suited to the atmosphere in the church, there came a lengthy pause as the song leader searched for the next number. Interrupting the deathly quiet was a sudden whirring, whistling sound that seemed to originate in the church cemetery. In ever increasing volume, the noise headed for the open church door, where it suddenly became a clacking sound and came down the aisle at about head height. *Clack-clack-clack.*

Unmistakably, it was the sound heard so many times there before— the sound of Aunt Het's teeth. And then suddenly those teeth became visible. Not only was the sound unmistakable, so was the sight. All in the church had seen Aunt Het's teeth before, and all had noted a dime-size yellow spot at the side of the upper plate. And there was that yellow spot on the unearthly teeth.

Having made the grand entry, the spectral teeth began to zip about over the sanctuary, as might a fly being pursued by a swatter. And almost instantly the teeth zipped straight to Flirting Marge and Luke, swinging back and forth in front of the terrified couple, biting each on the nose again and again. Flirting Marge fell back in a faint, while Luke sailed like a flying squirrel through the nearest window. He later stated that an eight-foot diamondback rattler nipping him on the nose would not have terrified him as much as being "hant bitten."

A stunned silence fell over the church, but only for a few moments. Then sheer pandemonium broke loose. There was screaming, shouting, jumping, and running all over the place. As happens in such extreme flight, all civility and concern for others vanished. Good friends and even family members clawed, kicked, and knocked at each other in the quickly clogged doorway, screaming, "Get out of the way, let me out of here!" Children were left behind in the mad melee; some of them had been sleeping on the benches, likely not for long when the uproar broke loose.

At first, the preacher just froze where he was sitting, but when the teeth zeroed in on him and whirred around him two or three times, he suddenly unfroze and lunged for a nearby open window.

Within moments the crowd had dispersed; few folks found the road—they ran in every direction, soon disappearing into the surrounding brush and pine thickets. A few even passed right through the graveyard in their wild dash to put as much space as possible between themselves and a set of ghostly false teeth, but in such panic, they likely never noticed where they were.

Well, it did take a while to get all the folks coming back to church again after that unforgettable Sunday. Even so, most of them for many weeks afterward sat on the edge of their bench, keeping a sharp eye toward the one door to the outside. Many years passed before night services resumed again. Seems that no one wanted to encounter zipping ghost teeth in the dark!

A Good Place to Learn

On a bright Monday morning long ago, folks in Bellefonte, Arkansas, gathered at the local store and post office to get their mail. A young local minister had preached at the Methodist church the day before, and his stirring, near eloquent sermon was the chief topic of conversation. The young man had, of course, been to a seminary and had learned a lot to preach about.

As the minister's aged grandmother waddled in to pick up her mail, one of the ladies present stepped forward, took her hand, and said, "Just wanted to tell you, Aunt Fannie, how I enjoyed your grandson's sermon here yesterday."

The old woman's eyes moistened a bit. She smiled and replied, "Why, thank you, Melrose. I'm real glad to hear you say that. It was a sight of a good sermon wasn't it? But land, honey, he ought to be able to preach good, for he's already spent two years in the cemetery!"

Could Have Been Better

Brother Robert Sheffey, a noted circuit-riding Methodist preacher and evangelist, long labored in the mountains, hills, and valleys of southwest

Virginia and adjoining area. He was well loved and highly respected by most of the religious folks with whom he worked, and many of the unbelievers had warm feelings toward him. An eccentric of the highest order, he did nearly everything different from the standard practice of the clergy, making him a legend during his own time. And though he has been gone for over a century now, the legend lives on.

He frequently was asked to render grace whenever he was a dinner guest, and his manner of giving thanks was indeed unordinary. As part of his unique prayer, Brother Sheffey always named everything on the table, even down to the contents of the sugar bowl and salt and pepper shakers.

About ten years before he died, he was invited to the home of a rather prominent and well-to-do family near Tazewell, Virginia. When everyone had sat down to the bountiful meal, Brother Sheffey was asked to do the honors. After blessing the potatoes, beans, cabbage, and other things on the table, he finally came to the meat. "Lord, I thank you for this extra big bowl of boiled chicken." He paused a moment before continuing, "Now, Lord, it's mighty good grub, but it would have been a sight better if she'd a-made dumplings with it!"

You may about bet that the next time he visited there, dumplings were on the table.

SURPRISE PRAYER

Webb Pierce, living in the rough mountain country of Giles County, Virginia, was considered a wicked man by his neighbors. He could out-cuss anyone in the county, and it was rumored that he was a part-time moonshiner. Widely known as an avid womanizer, he had been in lots of fights, and many suspected him of having murdered the husband of a lady he'd been visiting on the sly.

He was antagonistic toward the local churches, and no preacher was welcome in his home. The few who had tried to visit him for the purpose of presenting the saving Gospel were ordered off the place, with threats of bodily harm if they did not quickly retreat.

In spite of his hostile and rough nature, Webb loved his sons and daughters; if anything, he overprotected them. Of the dozen or so children that filled his large but crude log home, his favorite was a son about ten years old. One day as the little boy picked blackberries behind the barn, a large rattlesnake bit him. His cries brought Webb and others running to his side, and they carried the lad home and laid him on the porch. The swelling quickly moved up his leg, and he began to vomit and become delirious. Nothing short of a miracle would keep the boy from certain death.

Webb had heard of the effective prayers of Brother Sheffey, the eccentric Methodist preacher mentioned in the preceding story, who was then staying in the home of a neighbor just over the ridge in a nearby hollow. In desperation, he forgot his animosity toward all men of the cloth and sent a grown son running for him.

In a short time Brother Sheffey rode up to the gate on his horse. He dismounted with his prayer rug in hand (he always carried a sheepskin to kneel on when offering prayers) and walked calmly into the yard, never saying a word to anyone. He put the prayer rug down on the porch by the deathly sick child, knelt down, and slowly raised his hand toward Heaven. "Thank God for rattlesnakes!" he loudly exclaimed. "If this rattlesnake hadn't curled up in that blackberry thicket and bit this little boy, this wicked old man would have never allowed a servant of yours to be on his place. Now, Lord, I pray that this child may live. But I ask you to send another—even bigger—rattlesnake and nip the shank of this badly erring sinner and cause him to repent!"

This story has a happy ending. The child was soon eating a hearty supper at the time he should have been on the cooling board. The father repented that very day and became a long-faithful member of the local Methodist church. Perhaps he didn't want to take chances with that bigger rattlesnake for which Brother Sheffey had so earnestly prayed.

THE ORDER KEEPER

My great-grandfather Joseph E. Cornett (1814-1891) of Crown, Kentucky, on Dry Fork in Letcher County, was another unforgettable character. Like Robert Sheffey, he, too, became a legendary figure who is still often spoken of by those who heard their parents and grandparents relate many stories pertaining to him.

I am fortunate to have known several persons who knew and remembered him. One of his granddaughters, the late Sarah Cornett Draughon Caudill, who long lived at Blackey, Kentucky, was partly raised in his home, and she shared with me priceless information about him.

He stood tall and lean, his bushy hair was long, and he wore a full beard. His squinty eyes were very piercing. His face showed kindness but unrelenting sternness. His feet and hands were unusually oversized. Indeed, his feet were so large (about size 14) that some folks called him "Big Footed" Joe Cornett.

In some manner he had obtained a good education, though he lived in a time and locale where a great segment of the population could not read or write. He wrote deeds, notes, and such for his neighbors. And near the end of his life, he penned his own will, later adding a codicil or two. His superior learning was such that he was once or more elected superintendent of education for his county.

Several old-timers told me that when Letcher County was formed in 1842, he helped to lay out the town of Whitesburg for a county seat. A little later he was elected county judge, and through the years, he was known as Judge Cornett. He was a staunch Democrat, but his older half-brothers were equally staunch Republicans.

While serving as judge, he also practiced medicine, including some surgery—thus he was also sometimes known as Doctor Cornett—even though he had not so much as ever seen the inside of a medical school. About 1878, he was elected county judge once more.

He was a strong believer in and a member of the Old Regular Baptist faith, which flourished in the area. Actually, in that locale, "other brand" churches were few. He attended the Sandlick Regular Baptist Church (organized 1815) about two or three miles from his home.

In religion, as well as anything else he earnestly pursued, he put his whole mind and strength. The Regular Baptist church held services only one weekend during the month. On Saturday would be a business meeting followed by a time of worship. The time on Sunday would be given to regular worship.

Sometimes in between monthly meetings, Judge Cornett, perhaps seeking a little extra spiritual inspiration, would call in his neighbors for a time of hymn singing. He dearly loved singing; indeed, he wrote several songs, one or two of which are still sometimes used in church services in that area. And those who love such sentimental ballads, which pass as hymns, likely sing them around firesides now and then.

"Little Bessie," perhaps the best known of his works, tells the story of a dying child. Many believe that he based it on the death of his little daughter, Easter. Recently I heard the song in its full length on a Whitesburg radio station.

His granddaughter Sarah told me of one of those hymn singings held sometime around 1887, when she was about five years old. He had invited several neighbors, seating them near the hearth in his large living room. On and on they sang those haunting Old Regular Baptist hymns, as the fire roared.

Bill Cornett, a son of the judge, doesn't appear to have been very religious, if at all. Somewhat a prankster, he thought of something that might add a bit of excitement to the otherwise, to him, droll gathering. As the hymn singing dragged on, he called Sarah into the adjoining kitchen and offered her a nickel if she would do as he instructed. Of course, the child quickly agreed.

As a rather long hymn came to a conclusion, little Sarah squeezed through the seated crowd and stood by the fireplace, right in front of her grandfather. Then came the usual silent pause between hymns. That was her cue. Looking intently at old Judge Joe, she loudly sang out:

> Bobbed tail rooster
> And short tail crow,
> Did you ever see the devil?
> Uncle Joe, Uncle Joe!

Some of the folks sitting there might have found that to be funny, but not "Uncle Joe." Yelling out, "Why, you little devil," he grabbed her and, as Sarah expressed it over seventy years later, "he walloped me good" right before his guests.

But that is not what I started to tell. One summer, likely about 1878, Judge Cornett rode over to Rockhouse Creek, not far from the present town of Blackey, Kentucky, for an open-air service held in the shade of a grove of poplar trees. Planks had been laid upon stacks of rocks to make seating for everyone. In those days and in that area, such gatherings were common during the summer months. Judge Cornett felt it his duty to keep good order on the meeting grounds.

This particular well-attended affair included many young folks of the community. The service continued for hours, which necessitated trips to a nearby thicket for many of the crowd, as no bathroom facilities were available. Doubtless many people used the trip as an excuse to escape the misery of the improvised seating arrangements, to stretch a bit, or simply to relieve the boredom of a too long and sometimes dull meeting.

Three or four girls, sitting together, arose and went to the thicket. They returned but went again about 30 minutes later. Returning once more, they took their seats and ostensibly listened intently to whichever preacher then speaking "at the stand." (Usually from five to ten preachers spoke, and all of them had to have their say, with no time limits!) The girls arose and started to the thicket a third time, but the old judge straightened up, frowned, and shook his head, saying nothing, but the girls went ahead anyway.

Then when the seventh or eighth preacher took the stand, the girls arose and started again. That was too much. Judge Cornett stood up, pointed a finger directly at them, and called out, "Land, girls, did y'all come by a watermelon patch on the way here? I declare, if I had a flow like that, I'd a-brought a gourd!" (A large gourd was often used for a chamber pot.) The greatly embarrassed girls went on to the thicket, but they must have kept going, for they did not return to the meeting ground.

Great-grandfather Cornett now rests in the Sandlick Cemetery near Whitesburg, Kentucky. He is largely remembered because he was different than most of his contemporaries. Take heed, all you who would be long remembered.

Uncle Ben Raises the Dead

My great-uncle Ben Cornett lived on Dry Fork, near Whitesburg, Kentucky, in Letcher County. Like his father, Judge Joe Cornett, he was a bit eccentric, but in a different way. For one thing, his father was super-religious, whereas Ben was very much on the worldly side. But he did often attend church. Unlike his father, who would worship only with the Old Regular Baptists, Ben visited many churches. He seemed to derive a certain pleasure from comparing the faith and practices of widely diverse groups. At first he had little choice—Letcher County at that time was just about all Baptist. But by 1900, and possibly a few years before, a few other denominations had begun to make inroads in the area.

It was about 1903 when a group on Dry Fork started holding meetings that were about as far as one could get from the Regular Baptist faith. They called themselves The Holy and Sanctified Saints of the New Jerusalem, though Crown on Dry Fork was a "mighty far piece" from that holy city. Among other things, they claimed to have power to heal the sick, restore sight to the blind, and even raise the dead, if God so willed it. As unusual as their doctrine was to the local folks, it appealed to some, so before long, the number of Sanctified Saints greatly increased.

Just below Ben Cornett's farm and up a little hollow lived "Short" Joe

Stidham. He opened his home to the "strange" preachers from Tennessee for their first protracted meeting (revival) to promote their work on Dry Fork. In a short time, that meeting got lively. Nightly, folks claimed to get "holy sanctified," while others declared they'd been healed of all manner of diseases. There was much shouting, jumping, and dancing, and some were "falling under the power" and rolling in the floor, which itself was enough to draw the curious of the community.

Joe Stidham's brother, Ned, lived in a smokehouse-size cabin a short distance up the hollow. He was unstable, to say the least, and could be talked into just about anything, especially when offered a dollar or two. He attended the meetings faithfully, except one certain night when he failed to appear.

That night, one of the preachers got up and announced that he had some sad news. Poor Ned Stidham, he said, had been found dead in his humble little cabin that day. The preacher went on to say that the body had been brought there to his brother Joe's house, where it was laid out in the back room, awaiting the making of a coffin.

Then he threw his head back, rolled his eyes around, and bawled out, "But maybe that coffin won't have to be made. I believe we can get enough prayed-down power here tonight to raise him up again. Do you believe it, brothers? Do you believe it, sisters?"

After a chorus of hearty *amen*s, the preacher then directed all to get down and pray hard for the resurrection power to come into their midst. Virtually all in the room fell upon their knees, and the house was soon filled with loud pleas and some praises.

While all that was going on, Uncle Ben eased into the back room to view the corpse. I suppose he wanted proof. After all, he had seen Ned that very day in the woods where they both were squirrel hunting. Ned seemed to be well and strong then. Indeed, at last glimpse, he was running up a steep hillside to where his dog had treed something.

The room was lighted by only by one small flickering candle, helping to create a deathly appearance. Uncle Ben took a good look, then eased back into the front room, where, by then, most of those who had been on their knees were up jumping, dancing, and shouting.

Over the roaring din, the preacher yelled out loud and strong, "I sure do believe that the power is here in such a mighty way that we can raise this poor dead man. Let's go into the back room and witness the greatest miracle that ever took place on Dry Fork or plumb all over Letcher

County. Now, don't none of you let your faith waver and weaken the power. Just believe, and you shall see the power of God right before your eyes."

Uncle Ben was a bit amused to see that many in that crowd did not seem anxious to go into the back room. In fact, they began to slowly withdraw toward the front door. They loved preaching, singing, dancing, and shouting, and could continue such for hours at a time. They could even enjoy supposed divine healings, but now to see a dead man rise up from the cooling board was a bit much. This they would classify with the appearance of a ghost. Nevertheless, a sizeable portion of the crowd fell in behind the preacher.

Suddenly Uncle Ben jumped up from his seat and planted his huge frame in the bedroom doorway that led to the miracle room. "Folks," he loudly proclaimed, "you all know that I was raised a Hard-Shell Baptist, and I reckon I still believe that way. And we never heard of nothing like this. Now, I know I don't have near as much faith as the least of you, but I firmly believe that I can raise old Ned faster than any sanctified saint or preacher in the whole world. I think that boiling water right there on the stove will do it faster than faith. And I'm going to pour the whole kettle full right on Ned's face!"

Uncle Ben had noticed a kettle of water steaming hot on the wood stove by the bedroom door. Having made his statement, he reached over and rattled the kettle as he lifted it from the stove. With the steaming kettle in hand, he made fast heavy steps to where the supposed corpse lay.

Ben's resurrection power must have been stronger than he thought. He didn't have time to pour boiling water on Ned's face. The "dead man" leaped up with a frightened yell and, in one motion, sprang from the board and sprinted across the room. Knocking down several who crowded the bedroom doorway, he tore through the front room. He found the front door jammed with some of the saints who had lost their faith, so he sailed through a window, breaking out the sash and glass.

That was the end of the Sanctified Saints of Jerusalem on Dry Fork. Though Uncle Ben had raised the dead, he had killed a promising church.

ANOTHER APPENDIX?

Bristol, Tennessee/Virginia, is widely known as a city of churches, and rightly so. But not all hold their services in prominent corner, soaring tower, brick buildings; some are housed in simple—even humble—structures. Many congregations rented small, vacant business properties, though the practice is not as popular now as in the early days of the town. The local citizenry at that time considered most storefront churches to be a bit offbeat, or downright bizarre.

In what had once been a small variety store or rummage store on Short Street in Bristol, Virginia, there long existed Clark's Chapel (named by this writer, a few years after it began, for Earnest Clark, the man who started the church). Every weekend, the little church held a revival from Friday night through Sunday. Preachers came from far and near to conduct services. Most of clergymen were Pentecostal, and each meeting was generally expected to be long and lively.

One of the visiting preachers, Watson Lively, certainly lived up to his name. The fiery Pentecostal from near Lenoir, North Carolina, spoke every fourth weekend, often drawing the largest crowd of any others who preached there.

Nearly all those who preached at "the Chapel" practiced divine healing to some extent, but Rev. Lively went further than most. Every time he came, he conducted a healing session, and then some. For you see, he was not only a divine healer, he also assumed the role of divine diagnostician—at least his common practice would indicate such.

Often during a sermon he would suddenly grow silent and raise an arm toward Heaven, as if putting up an antenna to receive the divine dispatch. After a short, dramatic interval, he would rush out into the audience, put his hands upon a brother or sister, and then loudly announce that the chosen person had a medical condition that must be prayed about immediately. Perhaps a brother was about to have a heart attack, or a sister was on the verge of a stroke.

The careful observer would have noticed that the diagnosis usually was of a disease that threatened, rather than one that already existed. This made it easier for the preacher, in that there didn't have to be any real healing.

And who could say but that his faith had prevented a disastrous illness? The prospective victim was usually quite grateful, and who knows but that he or she might have put a little more folding money in the collection plate because of the supposed deliverance from impending calamity.

One of the most faithful attendants at Clark's Chapel was old sister Meldora Sutton, who lived on Second Taylor Street. She was markedly corpulent, yet near meeting time, she waddled down the street toward the little storefront church. She always sat upon a somewhat flimsy bench that sagged under her extreme weight. Few sat on that bench with her, being much afraid that it would suddenly snap at any time.

Though Sister Sutton was devout, she did not engage in the antics that often erupted during services. Instead, she just sat quietly, taking in whatever was going on. In contrast to many in such meetings, she was a sincere, dedicated, quietly trusting Christian. And she was extremely honest, a fact that would cause much embarrassment to Rev. Lively, as we shall shortly see.

One Saturday night he suddenly halted his sermon, put up his "antenna," and stood silently for a few moments, as if waiting for a heavenly message to come through. Then he made a beeline for Sister Sutton. With a look of surprise and compassion on his face, he threw his hands upon her head and declared that he must pray for her at once, for a revelation concerning a bad, life-threatening condition had just come through from God. "Your appendix is badly infected, is now swelling, and will burst at any moment!" he called out.

Audible gasps came from all over the congregation, and not a few folks appeared to be a bit embarrassed. Shocked looks passed between some, as they awaited the next development.

The old woman seemed to wrestle for a moment between her desire to always be perfectly honest, and another desire to spare the preacher from what she knew would be certain embarrassment. Honesty quickly prevailed. Looking up at the "divine diagnostician," she meekly but clearly said, "Preacher, I don't reckon that can be, unless I growed another one." Sister Sutton's appendix had been removed about a year before that time, and most of the assembly knew it.

The service instantly went "flat dead," as one who was present described it. Rev. Lively barely finished his sermon and immediately left without saying a "bye ye well" to anyone. He never appeared at Clark's Chapel again. And almost certainly, wherever he preached after that, he no longer gave a diagnosis of impending appendix disaster!

HE REMEMBERED THE DAYS

It was revival time, and the Calls Ridge Church was crowded. Folks had come from all over that section of Wilkes County, North Carolina, to witness the lively proceedings. The pastor, an elderly man with failing hearing, was nevertheless enjoying the loud singing, and he didn't have to strain to hear the high-volumed, zealous evangelist from over in Happy Valley.

Hamp Spicer, also aged, sat in the front and near a window so he could empty his well-processed tobacco juice now and then. A faithful attendant of the church, he did sometimes pray in public—but only when he was of a mind to, which was not often.

That night the pastor decided he would like to hear Hamp pray a little, so he duly called upon the old man for the closing prayer.

Hamp mumbled, "I beg to be excused," but he had a load of juice about ready for the window, so his speech was not clear and came out as, "Ise bay ta ba tused."

The minister looked long at him, somewhat shocked and bewildered, for he had heard, "I backslid Tuesday." After someone else closed the service, the minister hastened to Brother Spicer and, kindly taking his hand, said that he was sorry to hear of his recent backsliding.

"Why, land! Who told you such foolishment?" the startled Hamp exclaimed. "I've done backslid many a time in my life, but never on Tuesday, as I recollect!"

AT LEAST SHE HAD TRAVELED

An expression commonly heard in the Regular and Primitive Baptist churches of eastern Kentucky is "Tell us of your travels." These churches believe that one obtains eternal salvation by a slow and progressive travel from nature to grace, and that during this time one will have strange and notable experiences that may include trances and visions, which are taken as evidence that the seeker is making progress toward the blessed estate. When the experiences are convincing enough, the "traveler" will be admitted to full church membership.

One bright June morning long ago, a large crowd assembled at the much-revered Old Carr Church near Cody, Kentucky, in Knott County for the monthly meeting of Old Regular Baptists. As usual, there was much singing of the lovely, lined-out hymns, and four or five preachers held forth from the stand (pulpit).

At the conclusion of the several-hours-long service, the doors of the church were opened for membership. A tall, gangly, gnarled, toothless, old sister from far over the hills and way down Flax Patch Creek offered herself for acceptance into that holy body.

The moderator (pastor) of the group called the church to a time of consideration and formally presented the sister and her request for membership. "Now then, sister," he began, "tell us of your travels, and we'll kindly consider your request."

She stood for a moment, red-faced and a bit nervous, but oh so anxious to gain admission to that prestigious hill country church. "Well," she drawled out, "I've walked plumb barefooted fer over eight miles to get here. I got up way afore day and swallered a sight of sausage and gravy and biscuits, fer I knowed I had a fer piece to go—and climb a mountain er two, at that. And jist about daybreak I took out up Flax Patch, and I done stomped a toe and bruised a heel afore I got to the mouth of Yeller Cat Branch. But I come on, and, blessed Becky, iffen I didn't slip on a rock as I were wadin' the creek, and bruised myself in a certain place. Then I come to the trail a-leadin' across to the head of Little Carr, and rat there I stuck a thorn in my foot, and it's a-hurtin' still. And comin' across the ridge I pert nigh stepped on a big ol' rattler that were a-sunnin' itself across the trail. It took a time to kill it, but I did. And comin' by Uncle Hugh Wells's place, I very nigh got dog bit, and I'm a-dreadin' to pass back by there. Well, I come on, and I made it jist as you'ns whar startin' to sang. So after a hard travel, I'm here and waitin'."

Her tale may not have been what the moderator had in mind, but at least she had traveled!

THE HORSE OF A DIFFERENT COLOR

Established in 1810, the Indian Bottom Regular Baptist Church (Independent) served the people of lower Rockhouse Creek, near Blackey, Kentucky, for about 180 years. Though the congregation disbanded around 1990, the old building (erected about 1910) still stands today, now the property of the Letcher County Historical and Genealogical Society.

For most of its long existence, the church met only one weekend a month and was typically Regular Baptist: no musical instruments with the singing, no Sunday school, no night meetings, and no revivals. And it required applicants for membership to tell of their travels, in order to convince the elders of their worthiness.

In later years this church became what its sister churches would have called modern or apostate. It held revivals, night meetings, and weekly midweek services, and it didn't require a tale of travels for membership. It did, however, continue the practice of no music accompaniment with the singing, and it never had a Sunday school.

The "conventional" period was long under the iron but kind hand of Elder James Dixon. As moderator of the church—a position he held from 1876 until his death in 1914—"Uncle Jim" highly favored the custom of hearing applicants tell of their travels, and he judged their worthiness for membership by such, rather than by a simple profession of faith.

His daughter-in-law Nellie Whittaker Dixon, some years after she married his son Henry, came before the Indian Bottom Church and expressed her desire to become a member, stating she fully believed that her sins were pardoned. Uncle Jim was pleased; he welcomed the opportunity of receiving his beloved daughter-in-law as a member.

As usual, sitting behind the pulpit in his tall ladder-back chair (facetiously called Uncle Jim's throne by some of the non-members in the area), he leaned forward and asked for a telling of her travels from nature to grace. Well, Nellie had traveled, or at least she thought she had.

She began by telling of a beautiful, but strange, vivid dream that had come to her after she had fallen asleep while fervently praying for the pardoning of her personal sins. In the vision she was walking along the valley road that wound along the North Fork of the Kentucky River near Blackey, when all of a sudden a fine horse galloped up beside her and stopped. The saddle was empty. Then an unknown power or force lifted her upward and placed her in the saddle. The horse began to gallop again. The farther it went, the faster became the graceful gait. Finally the horse left the ground and flew upward and on upward, until Nellie found herself high among the stars and going higher when the dream ended. She closed by vowing that she fully believed she almost went to sweet Heaven but must wait a few years before finishing her journey.

Most of those present that day thought that surely such a grand experience would gain admission to the membership. They all could tell that Uncle Jim was impressed. He sat for a long moment with his eyes closed, deeply pondering what he had heard, then suddenly straightened up in his chair and leaned forward. "Now tell me, Nellie, honey," he said, "what color was that horse?"

"Oh, Daddy Dixon," Nellie quickly replied, "it was the shiniest, sleekest black I ever saw."

Uncle Jim slumped back in his chair, disappointment clearly showing in his troubled face. Then slowly and sadly he issued his decree. "Nellie, it makes me so sorrowful to tell you, but I don't believe a black horse is a holy horse, so we can't let anyone in this church on that color. Now, if that horse had been white, we would gladly receive you."

I am happy to report that a few years later Nellie Whittaker Dixon was received into the membership at Indian Bottom. And if it was "on a horse" I am sure that it was white!

THE UNWELCOME GREETINGS

The following two incidents, though almost identical, happened years apart and in widely separated localities.

In the summer of 1948, a big revival was held in the Assembly of God church at Moreland, Arkansas, in Pope County. Don Duvall, the 18-year-old evangelist had just begun to make his mark in the local churches. Henry Madden, the young man's well-known uncle, was not a practicing Christian, but he faithfully attended church. Though he lived several miles from Moreland, he came to the meetings to hear his nephew preach.

Henry, a confirmed alcoholic, had been "in Dutch" with the law several times in the nearby county seat town of Russellville. One night, as a large crowd gathered at the church, the uncle and nephew stood near the front door conversing. Up walked Tandy Verlin, a local bachelor, who was also a heavy drinker. Smiling in recognition—and right before the assemblage and highly embarrassed uncle and nephew—he loudly exclaimed, "Well iffen it ain't old Henry Madden! Land, I ain't seen you since we was in the Russellville jail together!" (I am happy to report that Henry spent the latter years of his life as a sober man.)

After many years on the evangelistic circuit, Duvall was in the midst of another great revival, this time near Greeneville, Tennessee. A slightly nervous and rather wild looking middle-aged woman attended every night. Then on Saturday night, as a large crowd from near and far gathered for the service, another woman of similar description slowly walked down the aisle. Looking around for a seat, she came face-to-face with the first lady. "Well," she cried out in surprise, "if it ain't old Jude Billings! I ain't seen you since we were in the solom [insane asylum] together!"

SOMEBODY TOUCHED ME

There was no other church like it in all the piney woods of south central Georgia. Known as The Sanctified and Holy Saints of the House of Jacob, it was another of those one-of-a-kind churches so numerous in parts of the Deep South. Some locals called the members Jacobites, or the Jacob

Wrestlers. The latter designation came about because one of their rituals, practiced when the members really "got in the spirit," was to turn out the lights and do a symbolic wrestle with Jacob on a large pile of hay that occupied the greater part of the middle of their open-air tabernacle.

The wrestle's participants included men and women, boys and girls. It had drawn sharp criticism from the most conservative of the community, who had noted that boys might be "taking hold of girls" before the lights came back on. And occasionally a man might be seen making sure that he got close to a woman, perhaps his neighbor's wife, before the wrestle began. But paired off or not, all the wrestlers looked forward to what they called the holy exercise.

No one seemed to enjoy the time of wrestling with Jacob more than the self-appointed prophet of the group, Buddy Ransom. He called himself Jacob's chosen son, who had been set aside to promote Jacobism in Irwin County and all over south Georgia.

Rev. Ransom (as he was titled, though he had no degree) had been one of the wildest young bucks in the area until he had done a stretch in prison for statutory rape. There, as he put it, he had "done got plumb saved and sanctified all over." When freed, he had come back home with a special mission of leading his former neighbors into the grand experience of Jacobism.

Strange or not, his brand of religion began drawing large crowds, especially after the hay pile was put in and Jacob wrestling began. Soon people were coming in droves from all over the county, the great majority of them in their mid to late teens and early twenties. And folks noticed that this segment of the crowd was the most enthusiastic of the wrestlers.

"Brother Ransom can shore draw the young folks," an old sister proudly told her neighbors. Well, something was drawing them, that was for sure. However, there did not seem to be a great increase in the spirituality of these young folks, but there was a noticeable rise in the number of unwed pregnancies.

In spite of growing suspicion and rather severe criticism among the more discerning of the community, Ransom erected a larger tabernacle, a hundred feet square. Though it resembled a timber shed, he insisted on calling it the Grand Tabernacle of Jacob. Most of its space was taken up by a gigantic pile of hay in the middle, and a four-way pulpit stood in the center of the hay pile. Two or three rows of rough, long benches surrounded the hay pile, but they were not capable of seating all who came to the meetings. When the call for wrestlers was made, many of the crowd streamed forth to take part.

Once the wrestle started, it would go on for an hour or more. Then Ransom would call out that the spirit of Jacob had retired to the heavenly home and that the wrestle must end. The careful observer might notice that when the lights came back on, several in the crowd had vanished—supposedly gone to the nearby woods and bushes to continue "the wrestle." Perhaps they wanted to wrestle until the dawning, as Jacob had done in Genesis.

In the community lived Gracey Perry, a maiden of 35 or so years, who always boasted that she was a pure virgin and fully intended to stay that way. "Why, no man has ever touched me," she would frequently state. "I don't know the way of the flesh, and don't want to know," she often added to her declaration of virgin purity. And she seemed to take pride in the fact that though most girls in the neighborhood were suspected to be non-virgins by the age of 16, she was more than double that age and still maintained her "holy chastity."

Though not a member of the Jacobites, she often attended their meetings. Many of her lady friends who had suffered from various ailments told her of marvelous healings taking place when the spirit of Jacob came down during wrestle time. They explained that there would be a gentle touch at the site of their ailments, and "sweet healing" would follow.

When Gracey began having female troubles, she asked a close friend, a zealous Jacobite, if she thought the spirit of Jacob would heal her.

"Why, shore," the friend replied. "Ye jist fall in the hay the next time there is a wrestle, cast your eyes toward Heaven, pray, and wait. I'm plumb shore ye will git a touch that will heal ye."

Gracey was a bit reluctant, but when the next wrestle took place—they were happening almost nightly by that time—she jumped up from her seat and hit the hay just as the lights were turned out. She noted that Ransom, who had been eyeing her a lot lately, hit the hay right beside her. Probably to earnestly intercede for her, Gracey supposed. She heard others rolling and thrashing about near her, as loud singing and pleas for Jacob to come down resounded throughout the tabernacle.

And then she felt it; a warm hand touched her thigh and slowly moved upward. "It's Jacob," she said to herself, "and he's slowly moving toward my troubles." And the hand did find her troubles, and moved about for a great while. And, yes, she thought she felt better—much better.

It got to where she felt that hand in the same manner every time there was a wrestle. Those touches from the spirit of Jacob were doing her so much good that she felt compelled to tell her sister Milly about them, even though Milly was a severe critic of what she called "the whole Ransom mess."

"He's still got the devil in his evil eyes," Milly declared, "jist like he did back when weren't no gal safe in a hundred feet of him. I thank hit's a plumb lie when he says he's done got sanctified from his red head down to his toes. I'd bet they's some territory in between that's still lack hit allus [always] was."

Milly's suspicions grew a few days later when Gracey came by and excitedly told her of her experience the night before. She had received not only a lot of extra-strong touching from the spirit of Jacob, but a heavenly message as well. She said that after much touching by the divine hand, a low voice whispered in her ear that she had been singled out for a special treatment. She had been told not to tarry long in the wrestle on the coming Saturday night, but to slip out to an old hay barn across the meadow back of the tabernacle. There she was to recline in the hay and wait. As soon as the spirit of Jacob had finished blessing those in the tabernacle, and the service was dismissed, he would come to her in the hay barn. He would overshadow her and give her a new and special treatment. She was further told that after her special new treatment she might even bear a holy child that would become chief among the Jacobites. The voice was thoughtful enough to tell her that this would have been done on Friday night but that a young sister of the group had been promised the blessed visit on that night.

When Milly heard the ridiculous story, her eyes flashed fire. "Is there gonna be a wrestle tomorrow night?" she asked.

"Why, shore," Gracey replied. "Brother Ransom seems to want one every night now. And, bless his righteous soul, he always jumps in the hay near me."

"Now, Gracey," Milly said, "don't ask me why, but let me rub yore thigh with soot before you go to that meetin' tomorrow night. You can wear yore extry long dress, and folks can't see hit."

Gracey always meekly obeyed her sister, so on the following afternoon, Milly raked out the cookstove and put the soot on good and thick.

Milly sat on one of the front benches on her visit to the tabernacle that night. Some folks were glad to see the bitter critic in the service, thinking she might have repented and would soon be a joiner. But she just sat stoically on the rough bench and waited in the dark for the wrestle to end. When the lights came back on, Gracey left the hay and returned to sit by her side.

Then Ransom took the stand to make closing remarks and to dismiss the crowd. He seemed rather anxious to close the meeting that night. Perhaps he wanted to "release the spirit of Jacob" for the hay barn visit! The night was extremely hot, and Ransom was already sweating from his exertions in the Jacob wrestle. He had hardly started to speak when he wiped his right hand across his sweat-drenched face. And, lo, there appeared a wide streak of black soot. He dropped his hand to his chest, and his white shirt became spotted black.

"See there, see there, Gracey!" Milly loudly called out. "See! Here's yore Jacob, and he ain't a heavenly messenger!"

"Lord Gawd, a'mighty," Gracey screeched out, "I's still a holy virgin, but a man's done touched me, and plumb up to my straddles. And a preacher man, at that."

Needless to say, if he appeared for the special treatment on Saturday night, "the spirit of Jacob" found an empty barn.

BLACKFOOT WILL JUDKINS

Will Judkins, one of the more prosperous residents of the lower section of Pierce County, Georgia, had the largest farm, the best house, and reputedly the most money of anyone in the area. And supposedly he had the "biggest dose of religion" of anyone in the church he attended. His father, one of the founders of that church, had sawed and donated the lumber from which it was built. And through the years, other members of the Judkins family played leading roles in the activities of the congregation.

An unusual ordinance of the old-fashioned Hard-Shell Baptist church was foot washing, which, along with the more prevalent Holy Communion, was done on Easter Sunday and again in the fall, customarily in mid-October. Of course, this affair was segregated by the sexes, with the brothers washing one another's feet in one corner of the church, while the women did likewise in another corner.

Indeed, segregation of the sexes went a bit further. There were two front doors (many old churches with two front doors may yet be seen today in rural areas of the South), and the men entered and sat on the right, while the ladies entered and sat on the left. This was done supposedly so that pious thoughts might be more easily maintained during worship time.

Foot washing, a symbol of humble servitude of one Christian to another, was not a time of real humility for Will Judkins. He always bought a fine pair of silk socks for the occasion, and, of course, he wore his best pair of expensive patent-leather shoes. This somewhat ostentatious display of prosperity caused a bit of resentment on the part of his more lowly brethren. And true to human nature, they talked outside the circle of fellow church members.

Among those who heard was a grown son of a poor member, and it so happened that he was a hired hand on Will's place. He conceived a plan to take some of the starch out of his proud employer. Just before Easter, he found his grand opportunity when all the Judkins family had gone to Blackshear on a shopping trip.

In Will's bedroom he found the black patent-leather shoes set out and a new pair of silk socks across them, all in readiness for the special service. He took the socks into the kitchen and put a generous supply of soot from the cookstove into both of them. He then carefully returned the socks to their original position across the shoes.

On that bright Sunday morning, the service began with the singing of hymns. After a long fervent prayer, followed by an inspiring and uplifting sermon, came time for the Communion and the much anticipated foot washing. And that was one foot washing that no one ever forgot!

Of course, everyone who participated made sure that feet were clean and the best footwear worn, but not all could afford such finery as that displayed by Will Judkins. Half the men sat down on a long, crude bench, while the other half knelt before them, with wash pan and towel ready. The order was then reversed, and the "washers" became the "washees." All went well until Will took off his shiny shoes and slowly removed the new silk socks.

He apparently didn't look down until the brother kneeling before him broke forth with a sharp and very audible gasp of surprise. You can hardly imagine Will's shock and horror when he looked down to see his feet as black as midnight! He sprang up and gave what some of those present described as a subdued yell.

Alas, one foot was already halfway in the pan, and that proved to be his undoing. The water sloshed out on the floor, making it slick as ice, and the pan served as a skate. The startled man slid forward in a curving pattern, while his other foot did a fast hop in order to keep up. The pan slipped over the edge of the raised pulpit platform, and the sudden drop of a foot or so jolted Will onto the main floor of the church. Sitting directly in his path was Narcissus Sullivan, who was as big and soft as a Georgia cotton bale. Will somersaulted right onto her lap and came to a well-padded stop sitting astride her, face to face, with nose touching nose.

In the commotion that erupted, many a person forgot the solemnity of the occasion and broke out in shrieks of uncontrollable laughter. Others jumped up from their seats for a better look at the unscheduled floor show. But it wasn't funny to old sister Sullivan.

She squawked like a badly disturbed setting hen. She didn't like that kind of closeness to a man, at least not in public, so she began slapping and pushing Will. Finally a strong push sent him sprawling over a short, backless bench in front of the pulpit, where he landed with his feet sticking straight up in the air for everyone to see. And believe you me, lots of "seeing" was done!

Will eventually regained his dignity and for many more years was a leader in the old family church. But he did one thing that his fellow church members could not help but notice. Though he continued to take part in the semiannual foot washings, he always came bare of socks, wearing shiny shoes only.

And he could never, hate it as he did, shake off the nickname that resulted from that unusual incident. For the rest of his life he was known as Blackfoot Will Judkins, and some even went so far as to call him Chief Blackfoot.

Foot washings are still observed in many churches throughout the Southern highlands. But if you plan to take part in one, be sure to examine your socks first!

SURPRISE IN THE OUTHOUSE
(OR MORE SMOKE THAN HE WANTED)

The old house and its nearby farm buildings look rather grim today—a picture of true antiquity. The plantation once known as Cedar Hill, but now long known as Painter Place, is a point of historic interest in the Holston Valley area of Sullivan County, Tennessee. Doubtless most passersby on Painter Road do not know that on the grounds of the austere looking homestead once occurred what I consider a choice bit of holy humor.

In the early 1910s, Painter Place was occupied by "Aunt" Caroline King Painter and her two unmarried sons, Philip and David. Aunt Caroline had a nephew (I think he was a Latham) who lived in or near Sarasota, Florida. She was quite proud of him, for he was studying for the ministry and showed much promise in that profession. During his summer vacations he came to Painter Place for a stay of several weeks.

The promising young minister-to-be had a secret practice that was frowned upon by most church people of the era—certainly by those fundamentalists in Holston Valley. He smoked. But he was careful to light up on the sly, perhaps in the barn or cornfield, walking in the woods, or in the outhouse that long occupied the southwest corner of the home's yard. Long occupied that corner it had, but it would not remain much longer after he came to visit that summer long ago.

Aunt Caroline had planned a little family get-together for him for the first Sunday of his visit that year. She sent word to select cousins and a few close friends to come to Painter Place for the afternoon affair. Most of the crowd gathered on the side porch and in the yard near it to visit and mingle with one another and later to enjoy a picnic-style supper.

As that long afternoon progressed, the young ministerial student's urge to smoke became stronger. Finally the craving became irresistible. He excused himself and nonchalantly strolled the short distance across the yard to the outhouse. No one thought anything about it, as someone often went to and from that necessary little building.

On the day before the gathering, Philip Painter had done some work on his nearly new automobile. Just a few months earlier, he had purchased the first car ever brought into the Holston Valley, and along with it he had brought a barrel of gasoline. (Service stations were almost nonexistent in the area at that time.) He had taken about two gallons of the gasoline from the barrel in order to wash some motor parts. After he finished, he poured the dirty, oily gasoline into the pit under the outside toilet, because someone had told him that if he poured the mixture on the ground, it would permanently kill the soil for several feet around.

The ministerial student went to the outhouse that day unaware that something unusual lurked in that unsavory pit. Once inside he decided to do two jobs at once, so he lowered his pants and sat down. Then he lit his cigarette. The outhouse was a two-holer, so he threw the still-burning match down the other hole.

Almost instantly there was a roaring *swoosh*, and flames and smoke shot up through both holes. And the young man shot up with them. In terror he yelled out and lunged against the door. The latch gave way, and

he jumped out into the yard, his pants down around his feet. He tried to run, but the pants hobbled him, causing him to fall forward. He instantly hopped up, desperately trying to pull his pants back into position. The flames rolled hot just behind him, so he bounded forward and went down again. The next time he got up, he kicked his pants completely off and tore out through the backyard gate, swiftly making for the cover of the toolshed.

The crowd, suddenly startled when they heard the wild yell in the outhouse, turned and saw the young man, naked from the waist down, jumping out into the yard. The sight of flames and smoke behind him greatly frightened many of them. Certainly the clear view of a semi-naked man must have greatly shocked the women present. It was long told that some of them just swooned away.

And while those women swooned away, the outhouse flamed away. Constructed mostly of pine lumber, it went up like a torch. The Painters got their water from a spring over the hill and far back of the outhouse, but there was no time to carry water to quench a gasoline-fed fire. In the excitement, someone did grab the big keg of lemonade and throw on the flames but to no avail.

In great embarrassment, the ministerial student left that afternoon for Florida. According to the late Philip Painter, the only real damage suffered by his first cousin was a "good singeing of his tail feathers."

Well, smoker or not, that young man went on to become a great Presbyterian minister, a profession he successfully followed for over fifty years. And you may be sure that he never forgot the time "when his sins found him out" in an outhouse in Sullivan County, Tennessee.

EXCITEMENT IN THE CHURCH

In the early days of Bristol, it was not unusual for the Bristol Methodist Church (now State Street Methodist) to have a little excitement. There was gleeful singing, lively preaching, and even a bit of joyous shouting now and then. One balmy Sunday morning in May 1878, the church saw some excitement of a far different kind than commonly experienced there. It was spirited but certainly not spiritual.

On that long-ago day, the singing had ended, the prayers were well on their way upward (hopefully), and preaching time had come. The overly pious minister had just opened the large pulpit Bible and announced his text when the front door swiftly swung open.

Was it a late visitor? Yes, and what a visitor!

Through that door came a young woman seemingly in a daze. Her outstretched arms waved about, much as if she were trying to fly. She swiftly proceeded down the aisle, all the while swinging her hips in the manner of a bawdy dance. To top it off, she was stark naked! She wore not a scrap of clothing, not even shoes on her feet.

The men gasped, the women shrieked, and a few actually swooned away or fainted. Some piously hid their eyes, while others stared intently at the strange visitor. By the time the first shock wave swept through and paralyzed the crowd, the naked woman had almost reached the pulpit. The horrified minister, seeing that none of the officials of the church were acting to remove this "emissary of the devil" from their midst, took matters into his own hands. He jumped down from the platform and seized the woman by the shoulders, intending to push her out the side door at the left of the pulpit.

His plan was thwarted a bit. The moment he laid hands on her, the woman pressed her body against his, threw her arms around his neck, and began kissing him. As one of the old-timers gingerly described the situation, "She blatantly with her body began to make the motions of sin. Now, with his hand on her shoulders it looked for the world like he was embracing her."

The shocked-to-the-teeth minister tried to jerk loose. While backing up, he stumbled on the edge of the platform and fell backward, bringing the clinging nude woman down on top, straddling him. According to the informant of long ago, "She there continued to do the motions of sin."

By then the good reverend was yelling for help. "Get this bawdy house huzzy off before she completely unsanctifies me," he begged.

By the time two of the stewards rushed to his aid, she had scooted upward and was rubbing his face with her swinging breasts. The stewards pulled her off the horrified minister and bodily carried her out the side door, into the yard. They quickly returned to the sanctuary, slamming and bolting the door behind them.

Needless to say, the morning service did not continue. Indeed, the minister, in a state of shock, had to be carried to the nearby parsonage and put to bed. The congregation scattered, hardly believing what they had seen.

Almost certainly, the nude woman was one of the workers in the Black Shawl, the notorious brothel that stood almost in the shadow of the Methodist church. Likely, she had been drinking or doping—yes, there was dope in Bristol at the time—or perhaps she might have been deluded by lack of sleep or from sheer exhaustion. In any case, her unclad visit to the church had long-lasting repercussions and was much talked of for generations.

The pastor was so shocked and humiliated that he could not resume his duties for well over a month. Some have said that he was never a very effective pastor after the incident.

The evening service following the woman's morning visit was a fervent prayer meeting to cleanse the sanctuary of the "evil" that had been so blatantly carried on there. One old brother prayed long and fervently that "the men and the boys of the congregation might have their minds blinded to the memory of what they had seen that morning, and that no vile and lascivious thoughts might ever arise in their minds because of Satan's effort to, in the form of a wicked woman, corrupt their morals and Christian virtues."

Though there was much righteous indignation because of this display of nudity and lewdness, some of the men and boys likely enjoyed the view thoroughly. Doubtless, many "vile and lascivious thoughts" centered on this scene for years to come. As was common at that time, for most of the men—even those who were married—the incident would be the only time in their lives when they would behold a nude woman.

The wife of the younger of the two stewards who had ejected the woman from the sanctuary accused him of taking a good look as he did so. Indeed, several in the congregation recalled that the older steward had turned his head and looked away as he performed his duty. They also observed that the younger man had "looked her over good," as his angry wife had charged. The distressed wife further lamented that she could not ever bear for him to touch her again, because his hands had been upon "that vile woman."

The most devastating and widespread repercussion centered on an elderly—perhaps the oldest—man in the congregation. His life and works were such that most Bristolians considered him a saint. Certainly, he was the most esteemed, respected, and beloved member of the Bristol Methodist Church. His hearing had begun to fade, and he had gradually moved forward to the front pew, where he sat when the visitor entered the church. Rumors began on that very day that the old brother had not covered or closed his eyes, as did many of the men present, when the woman pranced down the aisle. Instead, some claimed, he quickly threw on his glasses and intently stared at her, even leaning forward to apparently get a better view!

As those rumors spread, the congregation became more and more divided. Many said that such could not be, and that the old brother would not do such a thing. Others vowed they knew it to be so. Some of them said they didn't want to believe it, but they had to believe what they had seen. Finally, someone asked the saintly man about it.

"Well, I don't rightly remember what I did," he humbly replied, "but I usually put my specs on when there's something I want to see right bad."

His statement didn't do much to help his cause. According to several old-timers, this issue came the nearest to splitting this church wide open as anything that ever became a matter of contention within it. Bristolians, somewhat facetiously, branded the two divisions as the Specs Methodists and No Specs Methodists. Some of the members became hostile if anyone dared put them in the wrong category.

In time, the Specs and No Specs Methodists came back together. Today the State Street Methodist Church stands totally unified and is one of the strongest congregations in Bristol, and many in the present-day congregation probably never heard of the Specs/No Specs division that threatened their church so long ago.

WHERE PROVIDENCE ENDED

She was a big, fat, jolly gal, and her passing my house always meant a cheerful greeting and perhaps an uplifting conversation. Extremely religious, she was a pillar of her little church in Bristol, Virginia. Her strong faith permeated her discourse, but there came a time when her childlike faith wavered a bit.

She lived near the East Hill Cemetery and from her front door could see a giant poplar that had stood on the highest point of that ancient burying ground for perhaps a century or more. Through the passing years, it had stood firm against many a violent storm. But late on October 1, 1977, came a storm that must have been somewhat stronger than those of years past. The great tree fell to the ground.

A few days later I was working in my front yard when this old sister came waddling down the sidewalk. Naturally our talk soon turned to the storm of the past Saturday. Knowing her little house must have creaked and groaned before the powerful winds, I asked her how she had stood the storm.

"Lordy, weren't it awful?" she replied. "Land, I jist walked the floor and trusted in Providence till that big tree fell, and then I didn't know what on earth to do!"

Healed by a Snake

The Fire Baptized Holiness Tabernacle—actually a small, crudely built, never painted, board-and-batten structure—stood on a narrow lot between a rough mountain road and a swiftly flowing stream deep in the mountain country of southeast Tennessee. Its board, trustees, and pastor were all crammed into one person, Rev. Comer Frost. What he believed, his people believed, and his ruling on any matter was final. Along with the traditional holiness teachings, Frost had added the practice of snake handling.

His snake-handling bit drew a lot of visiting nonmembers. Not because they wanted to handle snakes, but because they wanted to see it done. Of course, the curious visitors took the back seats in the small building, but they still had a good view of the "show."

The valley was "working alive" with copperheads, so Frost had no difficulty obtaining snakes for use in his services. And a little farther up the mountains were ledges where he occasionally picked up rattlesnakes, some of them near giant size. Frost claimed that the Lord revealed to him where poisonous snakes could be found.

During a sermon one time, he suddenly stopped, raised a hand over his head, and proclaimed that the Lord had sent word of a huge copperhead coiled up under the front steps of the tabernacle. He marched out and soon returned with a yard-long snake of that variety around his neck. This helped to make believers of some who had been strong doubters. (However, others thought he had hidden the big snake outside in preparation for his display of divine revelation.)

During another service, the supposedly faith-filled preacher played around with a six-footer. But when the snake began to exhibit some rather pronounced signs of hostility, he threw it away from him and it slithered out the back door. Made folks afraid to walk home that night along narrow trails through the dense brush.

On occasion he would "give out" (a local expression for announce) a healing meeting. At such times he often had a larger crowd than usual. One healing meeting was set for a bright, balmy, late September Sunday afternoon. Several persons showed up for a touch from the "divine healer," hoping, of course, for complete cure. Among them was "Aunt"

Fannie Huff, who lived perhaps a quarter of a mile upstream from the tabernacle.

About three years earlier she had developed leg trouble of some type and had not taken a step since. The afternoon of the meeting, her daughter and son-in-law set her wheelchair in the back of an ancient, battered pickup truck and brought her to the tabernacle, where they placed her wheelchair in an open space that a heating stove occupied during the winter months.

After lots of spirited singing and praying, Frost took the stand. Peering over his dime-store glasses, he shrilly piped out, "Folks, we've come here for a healin' meetin', but the Lord has revealed to me that we ought to first have a provin' of our faith. And they's not any better way to do it than to take up serpents. Now, good folks, I's done gathered up a sight of snakes—thank they's about three dozen big ol' copperheads in our snake box. That's 'bout enough to go aroun', I thank. They's one big ol' rattler in here, and I thank he ought to go to that Baptist preacher visitin' from over at Gum Springs."

But the Baptist preacher had fled out the side door. Undaunted, Frost threw the big rattler around his neck and, with an armload of copperheads, started down the aisle. No one knew who would receive the big rattler. Of course, Frost had few to choose from. Most of the unbelievers on the back benches had suddenly decided that they'd rather be out enjoying that fine Sunday afternoon than to have their faith tried by a fanatical, wild-eyed preacher, and they seemed anxious to start enjoying the balmy out-of-doors.

Then the preacher reached Aunt Fannie Huff in her wheelchair. He stopped, looked straight at her, and said, "Oh, Aunt Fannie, the Lord done told me to try your faith real good, and iffen ye stand this test, I bound [bet] ye, healing will strike you."

Within seconds he stripped the big rattler from around his neck and threw it into the old woman's lap, where the snake wound itself into a coil.

That did it! Waving her arms about, Aunt Fannie drew back, too terrified to scream. She gave one big twist and leaped out of her wheelchair, sending the rattler under the bench just ahead of her. And that wasn't her only leap. To her side was an open window. In two or three springing leaps, she sailed through that window, hit the ground running, and didn't stop until she'd reached the porch of her home.

In the remaining 12 years that she lived, she never needed a wheelchair again. Well, isn't there a record in the Bible of folks who looked upon Moses' brazen serpent and became whole? Now, that serpent in Aunt Fannie's lap wasn't made of brass, but it got the job done anyway!

And that wasn't all. A fat old gal, frozen in terror by a copperhead that Frost had cast around her neck, sat on the bench above where the rattler had landed. That big snake wrapped around one of her millpost-style legs and began angrily rattling. That unfroze her. Yelling to high heaven, she jumped up, dragged or kicked the snake loose, stripped the copperhead from around her neck (at least she had now handled snakes), then tore down the aisle toward the front door. She lunged into Frost from behind, knocked him facedown among several copperheads that had been flung from the laps of the fleeing crowd, tromped over him, and sailed out the front door.

I don't rightly know what happened to Rev. Comer Frost. No one remained to make a report!

WATCH AND PRAY

The congregation of Sinking Springs United Methodist Church in the Holston Valley near Bristol, Tennessee, recently moved to a new building that was erected a short distance from the original site. Years ago at the previous location was a faithful attendant known simply as Sister Slater to most of the members. The devout old lady usually spoke only when spoken to, and every Sunday morning she quietly walked to the fourth row down. After taking the aisle seat, she bowed her head, closed her eyes, and had a long period of silent prayer.

The homemade pews had no arms and might better be called benches. The three back rows were usually the domain of the young folks of the church, and some of them were a bit rowdy. One Sunday morning those three benches filled to capacity early, causing several of the youngsters to about fill up the fourth bench where Sister Slater usually sat. But there was a tiny bit of room left beside the center aisle, and there she squeezed in when she finally arrived. As usual, she bowed her head, closed her eyes, and began her period of silent prayer.

Shortly one of the boys on the third bench reached through the slat in front of him and goosed a girl sitting there. She jumped sidewise, knocking the girl sitting by her over a bit. The chain reaction quickly spread down the bench until it reached the girl sitting next to Sister Slater. That girl also lunged sidewise and sent the praying woman sprawling into the aisle.

Sister Slater fell backwards, and her dress slid too high for her modesty to be served. She sprang up, apparently bent on fleeing, and ran down the aisle toward the pulpit until she saw that she was headed in the wrong direction. Then she whirled around and made a beeline for the front door. She never set foot in that church again.

One old fellow in that congregation opined that Sister Slater had likely learned to watch as well as pray.

ARRESTING A PAIR OF BOOTS

This may be a case of nationwide uniqueness. After all, how many attempted boot arrests do you know about?

Central Christian Church of Bristol, Tennessee, practices baptism by immersion. The church has an inside baptistery, back of which are dressing rooms for the officiating minister and those about to be baptized. The booths have doors like those often seen in public restrooms, that is, with an open space at the bottom.

The minister owned a waterproof baptismal outfit, similar to a rubberized pair of pants with boots. To make it more convenient for himself, he always left his outfit in the changing room, ready for the next usage.

Some time ago, a church member left an item, perhaps a book, in the church, and did not miss it until he arrived home. The young man needed it, so he returned and found every door locked. Undaunted, he searched around until he discovered a basement window with the safety latch open. He raised the window, crawled in, found his desired article, and left by a door that he could open from the inside without a key.

A neighbor saw the boy crawling in and immediately called the police. Soon a couple of policemen arrived, unaware that the boy had already gone, and began a diligent search of the large building. It was a time-consuming and frustrating task to check out the many rooms. Finally they came to the baptistery and switched on a light. Eureka, they found the burglar—or so they thought.

With guns drawn and aimed at the door of the minister's dressing room, they commanded the burglar to come out with his hands up. There was no response. A little louder, they gave another command to surrender. Again, no response. The officers told the burglar that he was covered, no escape was possible, and he'd better come out. He didn't.

While one policeman aimed his gun at the door, the other approached from the side, grabbed the knob, and quickly threw the door open. There they saw the minister's baptismal boots with the pants crumpled down on top of them!

I have always said that if a thing can happen, it has happened in Bristol. And this is one thing that may have never happened anywhere else.

In the CEMETERY

An epitaph, according to *Webster's Third New International Dictionary, Unabridged,* is "an inscription on or at a tomb or a grave in memory or commendation of the one buried there." Indeed, the word comes from the Greek *epitaphios* ("epi," meaning over, plus "taphos," meaning tomb or funeral).

You can find many books of strange epitaphs, many of them repetitions and most of them pertaining to New England or to Britain. In this chapter I have made an effort to gather epitaphs—most of them from the Deep South—that have never before appeared in print. Admittedly, Dixie does not have as many strange epitaphs as New England, but I have been fortunate to locate several, and I am yet on the lookout for others.

I have spent so much time strolling through Southern graveyards that some folks have facetiously called me "the man who dwells among the tombs." While dwelling among the tombs, I have discovered that not all tombstone inscriptions are of the sad, sentimental type. Carved in stone, these everlasting words are often witty, sometimes near bizarre, and occasionally brazenly frank. Some try to preach a bit, while others are judgmental, even to the point of consigning the deceased to hell. Some seek to share a philosophy or promote a political party, and a few almost fall into the realm of advertising. Occasionally the manner of death is described, sometimes in vivid detail. Some tombstones reveal the occupation or lifestyle of the deceased.

Most of the cemeteries I visited were public, kept in good condition, and near a highway upon which I chanced to be traveling. But if I spent some time in a given locality, which I often did, I sought old, little-used, and perhaps completely deserted burying grounds off the main highways or well-traveled side roads. These proved to be the most fertile ground for unusual epitaphs. I also found that the graveyards close by old country churches were likely places for finding out-of-the-ordinary tombstone inscriptions.

In several cases I was able to gain information as to how a strange inscription came about by making inquiry in the communities and towns where such were found. Amazingly, events often transpired to lead me to the right person or persons who could supply the needed details. Actually I do not regard this as merely a string of fortunate coincidences. Rather, I feel that they were the workings of that amazing synchronicity orchestrated by the Great Force that pervades all things.

One of the best examples occurred when I stood greatly puzzled, looking at an inscription on a stone in an almost deserted family cemetery in Abbeville County, South Carolina. At that moment a car bearing a California license plate drew up at the broken-down gate of that little graveyard. Out stepped an old but sprightly gentleman (I later learned he was 85) who had come to visit the graves of his parents. When I mentioned the odd inscription I was studying, he immediately told me that it was on the tombstone of an uncle of his. He went on to tell the long story behind it.

More than likely, no other person could have solved that mystery for me. In another fifteen minutes, I would have been gone. I could have been there much earlier that day. As it was, we were both in the right place at the right time.

A tourist attraction made up of unusual tombstone inscriptions could prove humiliating to relatives and friends of the deceased. Embarrassment has led some folks to cover inscriptions in some manner or sand them off. For that reason, I have listed only counties or, in some cases, larger designated sections of a state. Occasionally those who guided me to the cemeteries requested this.

I found many of these inscriptions in small, family burial plots located on private property, including a few places I would not advise anyone to seek out and explore. They are located in jungle-like brush thickets or heavily wooded areas that may be infested with poisonous snakes or unavoidable patches of poison ivy.

But I have endured the dangers for you. I copied the epitaphs, and you can now enjoy them in the safety of your home. The first one is the one that got me hooked.

WAS SHE A BAD COOK?

While wandering through a small public cemetery in Tishomingo County, Mississippi, in 1959, I found an epitaph that raised a question in my mind. I wondered if it had been written by a husband who had to endure bad cooking all his married life.

Helen Cook Baker

1876-1919

She was a Cook and married a Baker,

But that did not a cook or baker make her!

The homemade cement gravestone was a bit crumbly when I saw it, and I am glad I copied it while it was still readable. So many of these strange epitaphs have been or will be lost to the ravages of time.

STRONG WISH

In eastern North Carolina, just two counties from the Atlantic Ocean, is what appears to once have been a much used community cemetery, but when I was there several years ago, it showed signs of many years of neglect. Not far from the substantial front gate that had all but rotted way at the time of my visit, I noticed a large and obviously expensive marker. Recorded on its face was a strong wish, but not the usual kind:

EPHRIAM S. DAVIS

Who was born in Currituck County, North Carolina August 3, 1850. My much beloved husband who was brutally murdered on August 18, 1879, by Chester Doggett, who died five days later and is buried three miles from this cemetery, and for whom hell is too good. Oh, that it might be made thrice as hot for him.

I was fortunate to find a granddaughter of Ephriam S. Davis still living within sight of the neglected cemetery. She told me that on August 18, 1879, longtime friends Ephriam and Chester went fishing together. Ephriam's highly prized dog, Bouncer—yes, she remembered the name often told by her widowed grandmother—trotted along with them to the creek, a mile or so from the home farm.

At the creek side, Chester stumbled over the sleeping dog and fell hard on the sand. In a fit of anger, he jumped up and gave the dog two or three hard kicks, which greatly angered Ephriam. Hot words ensued, leading to a violent fight. Chester finally managed to draw his pocketknife and cut Ephriam's throat from ear to ear.

Within minutes, Ephriam bled to death. Chester dragged the body to a fallen sycamore in a nearby swamp and covered it with sand. In a short while, he arrived at Ephriam's home and told that his friend had walked into the swamp and disappeared, implying that perhaps he had perished in one of the pits of quicksand in the swamp.

Over the next five days an intensive search was carried on in the vast swamp, without success. On the fifth day, the searchers took along Ephriam's dog. When Bouncer reached the sycamore, the dog sniffed around and began howling, arousing suspicions of the searchers, who soon uncovered the body. The gaping slash of the poor man's throat was still visible.

Chester, who was among the searchers, quickly fled into the dense swamp, hotly pursued by angry neighbors. Late that day they found him, badly swollen and delirious, in a clump of bushes where he had apparently tried to hide. Two large cottonmouth moccasins were found nearby. Apparently the poisonous snakes had bitten him after he intruded into their lair. He died within minutes after the discovery.

Before either body was buried, Chester's wife confessed that her husband had told her the details of his crime. It had bothered her conscience night and day, and now that he was gone, she felt free to tell the story.

The granddaughter closed by saying that her grandmother always believed that the snakes were used to bring Chester to justice. And it was during the grandmother's time of extreme grief and bitterness that she had the revealing epitaph inscribed on the marker at her late husband's grave.

STRONG FEAR

In an abandoned family cemetery high on a hill in Ashe County, North Carolina, I came across a store-bought but modest monument to a man who died while breaking the eighth commandment. The epitaph expresses a strong fear for his eternal destiny:

> He fell to his death while stealing cherries from a tall tree.
> His bruised body lies here, and it is feared that his soul went to hell.

I could find no one who would talk about it, though 55 years had passed since the accident occurred. I suspected that the ones of whom I made inquiry were protecting a family secret.

STRONG POSSIBILITY

Perhaps the person who erected a marker in a little family cemetery in Madison County, Mississippi, was not sure of the deceased man's eternal destiny but felt there was a strong possibility that he didn't pass the final judgment. Still clearly legible when I saw it after a half century of exposure to the elements, it reads:

> He lived, he learned, he loved.
> But one thing he didn't do;
> He made no plans for that above.
> I think he went to hell—don't you?

Inquiry in the neighborhood yielded no further information.

STRONG IMPLICATION

Whoever erected this marker in Floyd County, Kentucky, did not exactly consign the deceased to hell, but the implication is strong:

> Buried here is poor Ned Still.
> The gospel he would never heed.
> He lost his brakes on a long hill.
> And met his fate at a mighty high speed!

STRONG STATEMENT

The old cemetery in Laurens County, Georgia, once served a large community, but as people moved away, the graveyard eventually turned into a virtual jungle. Many of the tall, once-proud stones had tumbled over, the fence had come down, and I saw evidence that stock from an adjoining farm had roamed over it.

In a back corner I found the fallen, luckily inscribed-side-up marker for which I was looking. It was crudely made of ordinary cement, and the inscription appeared to have been made with a nail. The man's first name and birth date had already crumbled away—the cement was obviously poorly mixed—but the last name (Poyntor) clearly showed, as did the death date (August 28, 1929). The poetry for the rather startling epitaph was poorly constructed, but its message was pointedly clear:

> My husband was a very wicked man,
> His dirty deeds I shrink to tell,
> Now that he has left this earth
> I'm sure he's gone to hell.

Upon diligent inquiry, I found that his widow, who lived "way down in Florida somewhere," had made the stone and inscribed it. My informant believed that the woman was more glad than sad when her husband—a notorious bootlegger, an avid gambler, and a compulsive womanizer—died after drinking "bad" whiskey. My informant also told that Mr. Poyntor kept his wife "well beaten." Now, that well-beaten wife seems to have taken her great opportunity to have the last word!

STRONG STATEMENT—STRONG WARNING

A strong statement joined a strong warning on a marker I found in an old churchyard cemetery in Tallapoosa County, Alabama. Several informed me the stone had been erected over the grave of a lonely bachelor who long attended the church that overshadows his grave. I also learned that the long-time pastor of that church, a zealous evangelistic type of preacher, erected the monument at his own expense, because he considered it a grand opportunity to preach to those who might look upon it in the future. (Perhaps he considered the expense as a donation to home missions!) Still clearly preaching its short sermon in stone when I saw it, it reads:

> We all long prayed for him,
> and tried hard to bring him to repentance,
> but he ever stubbornly refused.
> Now he is dead and has gone to hell.
> Let this be a warning
> to all stubborn sinners who may pass by.

STRANGE PRONOUNCEMENT

Much simpler and shorter than the previous message is a strange pronouncement on a low grave marker in a small cemetery at the edge of a large swamp in Arkansas County, Arkansas. When I saw the stone several years ago, it was fast crumbling and has likely now melted into the earth. The barely legible name appeared to be Weston McDougal, and the date looked to be 1890 or 1899. Beneath the vital statistics was the short epitaph:

> He danced his way into hell.

How I would love to know the story behind that short pronouncement. Was the person who wrote it a foe of dancing? Did McDougal die in a brawl at a dance or perchance drop dead on the dance floor? (I once had a cousin who died suddenly while playing dance music.) Perhaps we will never know, but that hasn't kept me from wondering.

UNCERTAIN FUTURE

High on a ridge above Clifty Creek in Morgan County, Tennessee, in a once-fenced-in, single-grave lot—only a post or two remained at the time of my visit—I found a homemade marker crafted from local sandstone, with its crudely engraved verse still legible:

> Here lays the body of John Henry Snow.
> The other day, he went away,
> To where we do not know.

Further inquiry revealed that many Snows once lived in the vicinity, but most had moved away years before John Henry's death in 1903. Some of them settled in Newton County, Arkansas. Indeed, I have a sister-in-law who descends from one of them.

A clerk at the courthouse told me several years ago that the area around the lone grave had become all wilderness and about inaccessible. John Henry Snow sleeps alone with future unknown.

SOME DOUBT

The few known strange epitaphs found in Oklahoma were mostly done in territorial days. In the woods at the end of what was once a cotton field in Muskogee County I discovered a lone grave. Whoever completed the epitaph for the small and plain monument had hopes but yet held some doubt. The inscription covering the entire front of the stone reads:

> Oliver McConnell
> May 12, 1860 – December 10, 1898
> He rested about all his life,
> and now can't do anything but rest—
> at least we hope he is resting.

SELF ADJUSTMENT

In Newberry County, South Carolina, I found a marker for Henry West in a brush thicket at the end of a neglected peach orchard. Most in the vicinity believed it had been erected sometime before his death. The thin stone had broken off near the base and was fast becoming covered by the soft earth around it. It apparently had been facedown for some time—the front was badly stained by the red clay soil—but had been turned over before I saw it.

Henry was born June 3, 1849, and died October 10, 1893. The epitaph, which he evidently composed himself, consists of only two lines of simple verse. Simple they are, but what great mysteries they may cover, and what great curiosity they evoke:

> I have a dark secret I will not tell,
> Now I suppose I will go to hell.

A local historian solved a bit of the mystery for me, or at least shed light on how the epitaph came about. When perhaps in his early 20s, Henry, son of a prominent and prosperous plantation-owning family, had become engaged to a girl named Alberta, daughter of another prominent and prosperous family. The supposedly happy couple went boating one Sunday afternoon on a lake that Henry's family had formed by damming up a stream. Late that day, Henry ran home with the sad tale of woe that Alberta had fallen from the boat into the deepest part of the lake. And try as he would, he allowed, he could not save her. Neighbors soon assembled and recovered the body before dark.

Within a month, the seemingly distraught Henry married another neighbor girl, arousing suspicions among the local people that perhaps Alberta had not drowned accidentally. Their suspicions became even greater when they later discovered that Henry and his bride had been carrying on a secret courtship for months before the tragic drowning. (It must have been a rather strong courtship, for a little less than six months after their hasty wedding, a child was born to the couple.) But suspicions cannot be used as evidence, so Henry lived out his days without trial or punishment.

After the death of his wife, Henry took up the life of a recluse in a former tenant shack on his portion of his father's plantation. He died about five years later and was buried in the backyard of that humble home. A few years later a peach orchard was planted on the property, leaving his grave undisturbed at the backside of the orchard.

But disturbed it may now be. When I later drove through that area, I learned that the orchard and all the land around it had become a new housing development. So Henry may presently sleep in someone's basement!

WARM AT LAST

Back in a mountain hollow in Haywood County, North Carolina, I came across what I thought to be a family cemetery. Nearly overgrown by trees and brush, the long-abandoned graveyard had only a few legible markers, and even they were almost faded away. One headstone bore a short bit of shocking poetry:

> He was so cold natured
> Warm in life he was not.
> Now it is believed he's very warm,
> In a place where it's very hot!

At the time of my visit, the poor man had been dead 75 years, and no one in the proximity remembered a thing about him or the family name (Winkler). I gave it up as an interesting mystery.

RARE FIND

While driving through northern Florida one day in 1974, I had been behind the wheel for several hours when I noticed a roadside cemetery. Since I was tired and needed to relax and stretch a bit, I decided what better place than an old country graveyard. Though small, it had a great diversity of family names, nearly always an indication of a public burying ground. Surrounded on three sides by woods and brush, the well-kept cemetery appeared to have been mowed perhaps that day.

In the southeast corner I found a lone grave with a small stone marker. Below the information that Nell Pruner had died May 2, 1936, was an unusual epitaph—and that is putting it mildly. The poetry for her epitaph—one of the few I have encountered that repeats the name of the deceased—is not perfect, but the message is there:

> Nell Pruner was a wicked lady,
> But she lived to be eighty.
> Here she lived long and well,
> She'll live forever down in hell.

Standing there fascinated by such a bold epitaph for a woman, I determined that I would find the story behind it. After all, she had been dead only 38 years. The name *Pruner* was nowhere found in the remainder of the graveyard. I thought that surely someone in the vicinity would know something about her.

I drove just a few miles into the county seat town and took a room. Then I began my search near downtown at a funeral home that appeared to have been in business for a long time.

"Sure thing," the balding, middle-aged, slightly overweight undertaker replied, "I know about that cemetery. Have buried several people there. It started out as a family cemetery—you likely noticed that there are several Reeders right in the middle of it with the best markers—but over the years, a lot of people were buried there from the surrounding area. One of the Reeders still keeps it mowed."

And yes, the undertaker did know about the strange epitaph. "Hardly have a burial there but that someone points it out to me," he added. "I could tell you a lot about it. My father told me all about it years ago. But I think you would do better by going back here a couple of blocks and talking to a lady who was one of those Reeders and was raised close by that cemetery. She can probably tell you a sight more than I could."

Well, I do not know how much the undertaker could have told me, but the woman to whom he sent me did indeed tell a sight about Nell Pruner. She told me that the woman had come into the locality about 1916 and bought what my informant described as a "worn out farm" about a mile due west of her final resting place. She paid cash for the farm, as she did for everything else she ever bought. She made no pretense about her past—in fact, she told everything in a manner that made local folks think she was proud of her unsavory former life.

For several years Nell operated a large brothel in Atlanta, closing it just before coming to Florida. Even though she was about 60 years old when she took up residence in the Sunshine State, she practiced some prostitution on her own after making the move southward. Then as soon as national prohibition became effective, she began what became a profitable new career in bootlegging. She was arrested two or three times but, for some reason, was never successfully prosecuted. Needless to say, she was not much received into respectable company in her new location, and she soon became a favorite among those of the lower degrees of society.

Not only was she into prostitution and bootlegging, she was heavily into the occult. Some called her a seer, others used the more common term of fortune-teller, and many called her a witch. Those who believed her to be the latter were greatly afraid to raise her ire, for fear she might cast a spell upon them.

Nell was noted for her success as a dowser, though she used no dowsing rod or instrument of any kind. If someone wanted her to locate a well, she just walked over the ground and finally would point at a spot and say, "Dig here," or "Drill here." Local folks claimed that she was never wrong. Some thought she had the power to move an underground stream to the desired location, but my informant thought this was mere conjecture.

More than once Nell successfully prophesied events that would take place in the locality. She once foretold that a fellow bootlegger would be killed in a car wreck while delivering booze. Sure enough, in about two weeks, he, perhaps having consumed too much of his product, ran off the highway at a sharp curve, hit a tree, and was fatally injured. After a well-known citizen of the area dropped dead in church one Sunday morning, Nell predicted that his widow would also die suddenly while sitting at her dining table two weeks from that day. She did, and that about made believers of all who knew about these happenings.

Nell plainly told that she got her power from Satan, saying she had sold her soul to his satanic majesty in exchange for her powers. And she would go on to say that there was no hope of her redemption and that she would certainly go to hell when she died.

About two years before her death, she foretold that it would occur at about 2:00 P.M. on her 80th birthday, May 2, 1936. She went into town and engaged the local tombstone maker to inscribe the marker of her choice. He made it as she directed, including the death date and the epitaph, and set it up in the little cemetery. In a time when most people in the region had empty pocketbooks, she paid him in cash, even adding an extra fifty dollars as what she called a gift.

All through the depression years, Nell had plenty of money. She was never known to have used a bank, and many thought that she kept large sums of cash in her home. A much repeated rumor stated that a local man of shady character, who had simply disappeared about 1931, had tried to rob her and that she had killed him and disposed of the body in such a manner that it was never found. Some surmised that he might have become food for alligators in a nearby lake.

In early 1936 she visited the local undertaker (the father of the man to whom I had first talked) and paid him the complete expense of her burial. She wanted no funeral, and she directed that the interment must be at sundown on the day following her death. She gave him a hundred dollars more than he asked, saying that he might as well have it, as the time would soon come when no one could enjoy the money she was leaving behind.

Soon afterward, Nell began to dress in jet black, seeming to be in mourning. She showed no sign of ill health or anything that would indicate an impending demise. Indeed, she went right on bootlegging and even planted flowers and put out a large vegetable garden.

In late April she sent the undertaker a letter telling him to be at the cemetery a little after 2:00 on the afternoon of May 2nd. The letter went on to say that he would find her body at the spot where she was to be buried.

My informant remembered the day, recalling that at about 1:30 that afternoon, she and her mother were working in their garden when they saw the supposed seer pass by. "Nell seems to be well," her mother remarked, "up and going on the day she's supposed to die." Both mother and daughter worked on.

The undertaker, who knew of the reputed foretelling ability of his client, decided to drive out to the cemetery "just to be sure." He still harbored doubts, but since it was only three or four miles out of town, he felt he had nothing to lose. Upon arrival at the cemetery a few minutes after two, he found Nell's body stretched out over the spot where her grave was to be dug.

My informant knew nothing of what had happened until the undertaker arrived at their home a short while later, asking her father and older brother to assist loading the body. (He had neglected to bring his usual helper—could this mean he did not expect to find a dead body?)

As directed, the undertaker buried Nell at sundown the following day. Though no funeral was held, a large crowd of the curious assembled for the burial. My informant remembered that an eerie silence prevailed. No one said a word; not even a discernible whisper was heard from the time the people assembled until they went silently away.

The flowers Nell had planted came up, but they were soon choked out by numerous weeds. Her vegetable garden suffered a like fate. Of course, there were those who soon went in to loot the house of its contents. But they left faster than they came.

My informant seemed reluctant to continue the story. (She had been a prominent schoolteacher in the local schools, and perhaps she feared that I would think she was a bit superstitious.) But she did tell that those who went to loot and perhaps to look for supposedly hidden cash were quickly driven off by the sudden appearance of a woman—supposedly the ghost of Nell Pruner—dressed in black.

NELL PRUNER WAS A
WICKED LADY
BUT SHE LIVED TO BE
EIGHTY
HERE SHE LIVED LONG
AND WELL
SHE'LL LIVE FOREVER
DOWN IN HELL

Nell left no will. Her place was later sold for taxes, but the man who bought it would never go about the house. (Perhaps he knew about the ghost.) After several years, the house finally rotted down, along with its furnishings. However, my informant said, hardy flowers still brighten the site each spring, as frequently happens in deserted home yards all over the South.

Before leaving town, I went by to thank the personable undertaker for his help in the matter. He asked if the lady to whom he had sent me told me about the supposed ghost in the cemetery. He then explained that most people who went to the cemetery alone would suddenly flee the place because of the appearance of a black-clad woman standing on Nell's grave.

He went on to say that the man in charge of the cemetery was having trouble keeping someone to mow it. "Just last year," he said, "a man left his mower running as he ran away from the place. He said he saw the ghost woman." In half jest, the undertaker added, "I guess you were lucky!"

Well, lucky or not, in that little roadside cemetery, I had found not a ghost, but the only marker I have ever seen that consigns a woman to hell. And it was a case of self-consignment.

His Trials Are Over

While wintering in northern Florida several years ago, I often passed the time by seeing the sights of that part of the Sunshine State. One day as I drove along a dirt road, I noticed a narrow side road. There on a post was a faded but still faintly legible sign that read: SHADY GROVE CEME-TERY, ESTABLISHED 1885. An arrow at the bottom of the sign pointed down the narrow road.

You guessed it! I lost no time in driving down that sandy, winding lane, soon to arrive at the double gates of a burying ground shaded by live oak trees. An abandoned church building stood nearby. I later learned it had long housed the Shady Grove Baptist Church, which had disbanded sometime during the Great Depression. Such old buildings and contents have a great fascination for me, so I looked it over before going into the cemetery.

Though boards covered most of the windows, the doors stood wide open. The floors were rotten and falling in. The ornate pulpit lay on its side near a window, and a rain-damaged pump organ still sat near an open window. The last hymn had been played on it many years before. Only a few broken-down pews remained. Most, I assumed, had probably been carried away to be used by residents. I did later see one on a side porch of a rather crude Florida cracker-style farmhouse.

I suspected that the cemetery was not often visited. When I opened the gate, its rusty hinges gave out a ghostly creaking sound. At first appearance, the graveyard contained nothing unusual, except that at least half the stones had the name *Garnes* on them. Near a back corner, shaded by the largest live oak in the grove, I saw an unusual marker. It was low, but extra thick, and seemed to be secured to a massive concrete foundation by two large steel rods. Inscribed in bold letters on the very solid monument was a thought-provoking bit of information:

> Here resting in sweet peace is John Thomas Garnes, who left this world of trials and troubles on May 19, 1930, at the age of 76 years and 13 days. During his long life he was tried and voted out of three Baptist Churches, including Shady Grove, where by the lies and baseless accusations of a bunch of hypocrites who were worse than he was, he was excluded from its membership. But thanks be to God, he was never removed from the Church Universal, and has a better chance of Heaven than did many of those who voted against him.

Instinctively knowing I had a story, I lost no time in seeking it. I drove back down the road a way to a battered old country store. Inside was an equally battered old merchant, who cheerfully greeted me and invited me to "take a keg and rest a spell." (Several empty nail kegs were used for seats on the front porch and around the big stove inside the store.)

When I inquired about anyone named Garnes who might yet live in the area, he smiled big and quickly replied, "Garnes, Garnes. Why, sonny"— I was then 37 years old—"they ain't much around here but Garnes. Them and the palmettos have jist about taken this country. Some of 'em are kin to me by marriage."

When I mentioned the inscription that had started my search, he drawled out, "Yas, I know all about that quare thang on that tombstone, That's old Uncle John Tom Garnes. I well recollect him. I used to go up to Shady Grove Church. Fact, I got religion there when I was about 17 or so. No preaching there in years, though. Some boys found a pair of powerful big rattlesnakes in hit here about a year ago."

Now, that was frightening! I immediately remembered I had walked through the shadowy building, over rotten floors and beams. And I remembered the patch of thick weeds that I had waded through to get to the front door. I shivered, but it was too late to be afraid! I knew I must pursue the story, so I asked for more information about Uncle John Tom.

The merchant replied that he could tell much more, but he thought my best bet was to visit one of Uncle John Tom's daughters, who lived about a mile away. "Why, old Aunt Nell Bivins down there is the most talky of all his folks," he said. "They's several more of his young'uns around here—he had 13—but Aunt Nell can tell you more about him than the rest of the bunch put together. I've heared her talk about him a sight, and you'll be lucky to leave afore dark, once you get her started."

I soon found that Aunt Nell Bivins wasn't hard to get started. Welcoming me as if I were one her long lost cousins, she invited me to sit down on the shady side porch of her rambling farmhouse. Before I was hardly seated, she stepped into the kitchen and returned with a quart-sized glass of lemonade as good as any I ever tasted. I was a bit apprehensive about asking her about so personal a thing as the church trials of her father, so I first just mentioned the strange epitaph that had brought me to her house. I hardly had to ask another question.

"Why, land, yas," she began. "Me and my man, Wilbert—he's been dead nigh about 20 years, I guess—had that stone placed there. It was hard times back then, and none of the rest of the family had any money, but we did."

I later spoke with the undertaker, who told me that Wilbert had been one of the most notorious and successful bootleggers in northern Florida, and that is why he had money when no one else did.

"I had that stuff put on his stone," she continued, "because I wanted that bunch of hypocrites up there at Shady Grove Church to know that Pap was still in the church that counts. Went plumb to Lake City to have it done. Cost a sight, but I's glad to do it.

"Now, I guess Pap were guilty that first time, but later I think the churches were wrong. When he was about 18, he joined over here at Bell's Chapel. That preacher over there at the time had a feisty gal—about 16 years old, I think. She got bigged [pregnant], and she accused Pap of being the cause of it. Now, by the time they had Pap's trial, the baby was done borned, and it were the very image of him. Couldn't deny it, they said. They throwed him outen the church over it. He wanted to marry the girl, but that fool preacher said he wouldn't have such a hypocrite for a son-in-law, and wouldn't allow it. The child they had is still living—a girl—she married a lawman of some kind, and they live over in Live Oak.

"Pap wouldn't go to church for years after that. Later when he was up around Jasper Baker's mill maybe—might nigh in Georgia, I think—he got his religion stirred up again. He went and joined another Baptist church up there. It may have been Sand Springs, not sure. After a while, they found out he went to a dance, and they wouldn't tolerate that, and Pap wouldn't promise not to go again. So they threw him out up there too.

"Then he come back down here, and not long afterwards he got real bad sick. Nearly died. That got him to thinking on religion again, and soon he come into old Shady Grove out here.

"Then about five or six years afore he died, they got a pastor that had a lot of quare ideas. For one thing, he wanted to be the whole ruler and not have any deacons—or at least they would have no ruling power. Now, Pap stood up against him good. As strange as that preacher was, he got a bunch behind him, and some of them told a sight of lies on Pap. Wasn't long till they throwed him and some others out."

Aunt Nell was really getting steamed up. I clearly saw that she was still angry, even though 40 years or more had passed since that trial had occurred.

"Now, sir," she continued, "that church never done a bit of good after that. It kept going down till there weren't enough to hold J. P. court with. And finally they just left it, and you see what a shape it's in now. They say some boys found rattlesnakes in it a few months back—maybe a year back, just don't remember. I can tell you they's some mighty sneaky snakes in it 40 years ago, and they had britches and dresses on.

"Some of them people didn't want Pap buried up there, but I'd'a buried him there if I'd had to take my Winchester along with me. And they didn't like what I had put on his tombstone. But I had that stone fixed to where the devil couldn't carry it off. But I reckon you done seen it."

Yes, I had seen it and I had heard all about it, and now I have written it!

Their Passions Were Strong

What we the living much accept is that those sleeping beneath the sod had just as strong passions when they lived, as do we who are yet alive. Indeed, we all are the result of a long chain of human passions that reaches back to the first male and female couple. Perhaps the records of the passions of most people tend to be buried with the body. But not so in every case. In my travels through the South, I have found a few grave markers that indicate that the persons they memorialize had passions stronger than most. Or perhaps they simply gave more vent to their passions than the rest of us.

Some of the epitaphs revealing the passionate nature of the deceased were clearly composed by family members who ordered the marker and dictated the inscription. Others appear to have been directed by the person memorialized before his or her death. Some may have an element of the last word type of revenge, as by a wronged spouse, girlfriend, or boyfriend. Consider the following tales.

DEATH COOLED HIM DOWN

In Evangeline Parish, Louisiana, I found a terse epitaph inscribed on a low, modest grave marker:

Here lies the body of "Wild" David Reece.
His strong passions cooled by death,
He now rests in peace.

Upon inquiry, I learned that his widow—his fifth wife—and several of his children, both legitimate and illegitimate, still lived in the area. "Why, his son David is just as wild as he was," my informant stated. "He runs a honky-tonk out here in the country, and it's a bad one, too." Among other things, the elder David Reece was a piano tuner. "Most wise husbands stayed at home with their wives when David was due to tune the piano," my informant added with a chuckle.

HE WAS NOT A SAINT

The tall, slender monument in a family cemetery in Columbia County, Arkansas, states the obvious—at least to those who knew Jonathan Bott. He died in 1896, and his stone was in moderately good condition with the inscription still clearly legible when I saw it more than 50 years later:

Here rests one Jonathan Bott,
Who a saint was surely not.
He had wild passions so very strong,
So was always out doing wrong!

In Magnolia (a sizeable town in that county) I found an older man whose father had known Jonathan and had passed a good deal of information on to him. Jonathan was what locals called a "drop shot," or one who just dropped into the region from parts unknown. Usually such persons never revealed much about their past. Most of them were suspected of having a criminal past, and some may well have used an assumed name.

My informant described Jonathan as a "kingpin carpenter" who had built several of the fine houses in Magnolia. He had taken up with a family in the northern part of the county and had lived there until he died, his past still unknown. But his present was known by most of the people living in that part of Columbia County. Indeed, he was always out doing wrong, as his epitaph clearly states.

"He would carpenter all day, and then court all night," my informant said a bit shyly. "A daughter of that family where he stayed—she'd been married but had come back home—had two young'uns by him. They both live here in Magnolia, but I reckon I'd best not call their names."

He told me before I left Magnolia that Jonathan's gravestone was "put up" by the woman who bore the two children. A bit peeved at him for not marrying her, she wrote an epitaph that told it like it was.

LONG-LASTING PASSION

Not too far south of Tupelo, Mississippi, I happened upon what once was a large cotton plantation with two burying grounds—one for the master and his family, one for the slaves and the ex-slaves who stayed on as tenant farmers. The plantation had been long sold and divided into small farms by the time I visited, and the family had all moved away.

I learned from citizens of the area that the "old master" loved some of his slaves so much that he had them buried in the family cemetery. He also erected markers at their graves, an unusual practice for slave burials. In the family cemetery I saw a small face-up marker with a startling statement inscribed upon it:

Thomas Blackwelder
Feb. 13, 1790 – Nov. 11, 1892
Here lies a good and noble man, who was a kind
and faithful husband to three wives, and whose
youngest child was 67 years younger than the oldest.

The marker for Thomas was similar to other slave markers, so I believe he was a former slave who had remained on the plantation. Deducing from information on his tombstone, he was at least in his 80s at the birth of his last child.

From Youth to Old Age

Wallace Croft, who spent most of his long life deep in southern Alabama, was a cotton farmer but not a plantation master. He was merely a tenant on a large tract. And from the statement on his marker, he seems to have had plenty of family hands to help cultivate his cotton fields:

> Here resting in the hope of a glorious resurrection is
> Wallace W. Croft,
> who was born in Georgia, December 21, 1825,
> and who died in Alabama, December 25,1917.
> He was married four times and fathered 27 children,
> the first when he was 15 and the last when he was 79.

I was able to locate many of his younger children still alive, and they all were kind, hospitable people who showed a pronounced fondness for their quite prolific father.

His Children Rise Up and Call Him Blessed

If perchance there are doubting Thomases out there who are skeptical of aged fathers, let me give you some examples from my own family. David Vincent Reddell (Riddle), my great-grandfather Reddell's half brother, lived on Dry Creek in Newton County, Arkansas. By two wives he fathered 25 children, the last born when he was about 75 years old.

My great-grandfather Maggard's brother, Rudolph Maggard, at age 59 married a 16-year-old neighbor girl (my great-grandmother's half sister). Their last child was born when he was 74 years old. I venture to say that there likely would have been more, had he not died soon after the baby's birth.

Isham (Isom) Caudill, my great-great-great grandmother Abigail Caudill Pennington's brother, was born April 2, 1789, in Wilkes County, North Carolina, and died 103 years later on May 18, 1892, in Letcher County, Kentucky. At the age of 82, he fathered a son, Hiram Caudill, whom I had the pleasure of meeting in the autumn of 1960. Hiram died in 1962, certainly one of the last—if not the last—persons in America who had a parent born in the 1700s.

Passion Led to Murder

In northeastern South Carolina I found an epitaph containing a confession of a dark crime. Many descendants of the deceased still lived in the area, but they were reluctant to talk of the matter. Several years later a local resident told me—but I cannot confirm—that the inscription had been sanded out of the marker. (I have known of this happening in other cases.) But for many years it was there, plain for everyone to see.

Richard Bernhardt was born in 1865 and died in 1922. Two wives preceded him in death and are buried by his side. The first died very young in 1887; the other died in 1920. The confession goes (or went) like this:

> Now that I am safe I want all to know
> that it was I who shot and killed Oliver Colton,
> because I wanted his wife, and I got her.
> She sleeps here by my side.

I went into the town and was fortunate to find an old lawyer who remembered Oliver Colton's murder. He told me that Oliver was sitting on his porch one hot night, when someone shot him from a nearby hedgerow. For years the murder remained unsolved, and folks were surprised when the strange epitaph appeared on Richard's grave marker. The lawyer remembered that the stone was put up by the administrator of the estate, as prescribed in the will. Indeed, Richard put a provision in his will that if it were not done, then the will would become null and void. Evidently he had a great need to confess—but only after he was safe from prosecution.

THEY FINALLY KNEW

Darthula Combs, who lived in central Georgia and never married, gave birth to five illegitimate children. She and her mother reared them to adulthood, and all of them married well and were highly respected citizens. Of course there was much speculation over the years as to who fathered Darthula's children, but she would never tell. She had a reason not to, as divulged by the inscription she instructed her oldest son to put on her tombstone:

> I want all who were so curious during my lifetime
> to know that Dr. David Wade who was my brother-in-law,
> and who sleeps five spaces over in this family row,
> was the father of my five children.

What eyebrows that must have raised in so small a town. Dr. Wade indeed is buried five spaces over from Darthula. His large double monument shows that he was ten years older than Darthula and had died five years before her death. His wife died when her younger sister, Darthula, was 16. From local citizens I learned that he never remarried.

Young Darthula bore a child within a year after her sister's death, and four more followed over the next 15 years. Her oldest child, a son, became a doctor in a large Southern city. Local folks had wondered how Darthula managed to send him through medical school. Doubtless his father supplied the money.

Darthula's revealing epitaph was also likely a numbing shock to members the local Baptist church, where Dr. Wade had been a deacon for over 30 years, even serving as chairman of the deacon board. Oh, well, there would be lots of shocks everywhere if the truth were always known. But rarely does a person put such shocking disclosures on a grave marker.

NOTABLE ACCOMPLISHMENT

"Upper" Bob Collins was born August 25, 1852, and died March 17, 1919. He lived deep in a mountain valley in southeastern Kentucky, and was so called to distinguish him from a younger man named Bob Collins who lived farther down the creek. Upper Bob's old double log house was still standing when I visited there.

. He is buried in a little family cemetery high on the peak of a steep hill—such burial grounds are common in that locality—and his epitaph includes a startling statement:

> If certain women told the truth,
> he was the father of 28 baseborn children,
> plus his 13 at home.

How fitting that his monument includes the words AT REST in large capital letters. His 41 children may be a record for southeastern Kentucky.

Bud Daniels, the gnarled old mountaineer with whom I was staying, told me that if I would go some two miles downstream from where Upper Bob Collins is buried, I would find another family cemetery, not on top of, but lying up a sharp spur (little ridge) of the mountain. In that cemetery would be a "fine" marker that would solve part of the mystery of Upper Bob's 28 illegitimate children. "That woman with that quare thing on her tombstone was a second cousin of Upper Bob Collins in the graveyard up the creek," Bud said. He went on to add, "I well knowed 'em both."

I lost no time in searching out the cemetery. The large tombstone cheapened all the other store-bought markers scattered about the fair sized burying ground. I wondered how the mountain woman could have such a nice pink granite monument, but I was more interested in reading its inscription:

Anna Jane Collins
Born September 21, 1858
Daughter of Thomas M. and Cordelia Combs Collins
Died May 22, 1932
She was a kind and loving mother, good to all, a skilled midwife,
and noted herb doctor. Though never married she bore nine children
by Robert James (Upper Bob) Collins, who kindly helped her to rear
them all to adulthood, and educated all that would accept his kindness.
Erected by a grateful son.
Dr. Samuel J. Tilden Collins, M.D.
Spring, 1936.

Bud told me that Dr. Collins was rich and lived "up in Ohio somers [somewhere]." That explained the fine pink granite monument. He told me lots more about Upper Bob and his baseborn children, but this is not the place to record what I learned.

HE OBEYED THE BIBLE

In an all but deserted small cemetery in Smith County, Texas, lies the grave of Jamison Rusk, nestled between the graves of his two wives, Rose (1860-1899) and Lucretia (1882-1925). His epitaph reads:

Here resting peacefully between his two very beloved wives is Jamison Rusk, whose Rose bore 11 children and his Lucretia bore 14, of which 23 yet live. He had 142 grandchildren, and numerous uncounted great grandchildren. He truly obeyed Genesis 1:28.

The Bible verse reads, "Be fruitful and multiply and replenish the earth." Under the epitaph, in larger letters, appears a Biblical quotation from Matthew 25, verse 21: "Well done, thou good and faithful servant."

DID SHE GET HIM IN HEAVEN?

Central Florida does not have many grave markers with strange inscriptions, or at least I have never found them. But I did find one in a little cemetery virtually surrounded by orange groves, and I suspect that it predated those groves. Of the 20 to 25 graves there, the ones that were marked bore the usual, mundane inscriptions. But on the gravestone for Patsy Drew, who was born in 1880 and died in 1917, was written:

> Beneath this marker lies all that was mortal of Patsy Drew, who ought to have been the wife of David Watson, who also is buried in this cemetery, but she was pushed aside by a blatant hussy who enticed David away from her with her flashy charms. I vowed that I would have David in this world or the next. Now we are both in the next.

Wouldn't it be interesting to know if she had him in the next?

"Marrying Jim" Jennings

In northeastern Texas, in a still-used, well-kept public cemetery, are two or three unusual epitaphs. But the real corker is on the flat slab monument covering the grave of S. James Jennings, who long practiced law in the nearby county seat town. Inscribed in that beautiful pink Texas marble is this revealing epitaph:

S. JAMES JENNINGS
August 31, 1900 – June 11, 1946
He was married eight times and was
divorced seven times. He dropped
dead in the doorway of the local
court house when on his way to
file for his eighth divorce.
He may be now where there is no
marrying or giving in marriage,
but I don't think he'll be happy there.
This monument placed by his widow
who does not much mourn his passing.

I reasoned that the inscription was likely ordered by an unhappy wife close to being the object of the eighth divorce at the time Mr. Jennings dropped dead. My intuition told me I had a good story here, and a second feeling told me that the best place to seek information would be from the local marble cutter. (After all, what marble man would forget doing a job like that?)

I headed to town and found the marble works without difficulty—it was on the road leading in from the cemetery and had one of the finest displays of beautiful monuments that I have ever seen in so small a town, including that flat slab that covers Jennings's grave.

The marble cutter—a big, burly, red-faced fellow sporting a heavy, sandy red mustache—possessed just enough solemnity to grace his type of service. He seemed a bit cool and reserved at first, but when he learned the purpose of my call, he warmed up quickly, becoming as cordial as if I had come to order a dozen monuments. When I described the pink marble slab in the local cemetery, he brightened up and eagerly began his story:

"Why, sure thing, how could I ever forget that order? Strangest I ever had, and more lettering than I have done since I began work here with my father over 40 years ago.

"That man, I knew him well. He was a big lawyer here, and he would have been a better one if he could have got his mind off women and marrying. He lived two blocks on in, toward the main town, and just around the corner from that first stop light up there. His eighth woman still lives there, but she's sorta soured up now and won't talk much about the past happenings.

"My father always said Jim—we all got to calling him 'Marrying Jim'— first married when he was about 17 years old. He got a girl in his school class to swelling, you know, and had to marry her. But that didn't last long. He married again when off in college. One of his teachers. She was a good 20 years older than he was. But after a year or two, her daughter, about his age, divorced her husband and beat her mother's time with Jim. They run off together plumb down to New Orleans. Down there she took up with their landlord, and Jim was soon divorced and without a woman again.

"Well, sir, he got his fourth woman in the damnedest way you ever heard tell of. He told me all about it when I was using him to get a divorce from my second wife."

At this point, I wondered if the tombstone maker was on his way to becoming a Marrying Jim! He continued, "Seems he had a good friend— another lawyer, I think it was—who was trying hard to divorce his wife. Now, he needed proof of adultery. Her man well knew that she would seesaw with about anything that had britches on, but he needed to prove it.

"Now, you know, sir, old Marrying Jim arranged to get her to his house, and his friend was hid there to take pictures. And he did get pictures of them just a-going at it hammer and tongs.

"Of course, the divorce was granted, and wouldn't you just know it,

Jim and her was married just as quick as they could. Think he bought the license the same day the divorce came through.

"I guess they lived together about three or four years. One day when he was over at Tyler arguing a case, that woman just loaded up his Cadillac and took off. He had two cars, but one was over at Tyler. Strangest thing, no one could ever find her. Some thought she might have run that car off in a lake somewhere, but why would she have loaded up her stuff if she was aiming to do something like that? It took a while, but he got a divorce again.

"Now, I think the next two wives were women he was helping to get divorces. He had a habit of trying to get close to women he was working on divorces with. But he wound up divorcing them too.

"Then he got a woman from over about Palestine—don't think he knew her well. About a year later, I guess she decided to get a quick divorce. She poisoned him real bad. He was very near to dying. I think he finally was taken to a hospital down in Houston, but he did live. That woman run off, but they finally caught her way down in Florida—Orlando I think. She got sent to the pen, and he soon was free from her.

"I guess he finally decided that he'd better get a well-known hometown gal. So he got a widow, one of his former classmates here in the school. Right well-off too. Her daddy was headman up here at the big bank. [I presume he meant bank president.]

"I don't think they hit it off too good, but they dragged along for a while. He got to dogging around quite a bit, and she finally caught him in bed with the maid they had hired who was living there with them. They had an awful time about that. After a few days of warfare, he told her he'd go right down to the courthouse and file for divorce before he did another thing in the world. She begged him not to—not that she wanted to go on living together. But she was powerful religious and didn't believe in divorcing. But he took on off down to the courthouse anyway. It was just about three blocks. He went walking, or those who saw him going said he was trotting.

"Well you know, sir, he went to push that big door open—it's mighty heavy—and he fell there in the floor, just plumb dead. They buried him up there near his parents. Not much later, that widow came here and ordered that marker and all that stuff to be put on it. She seemed to me to be glad that he had died, so her religion was not gone against by divorcing. I try to please my customers, so I did it just the way she said. His brothers and sisters bucked some about it, but didn't do much good."

Then he added a thought-provoking statement: "You know, I sort of admire folks who express themselves no matter what others think."

I drove away thinking much on that statement, and do to this very day.

AT LEAST SHE TRIED

Once while driving through Wilkes County, Georgia, I stopped at an old country church set a way back from the road. Farther back I found a burial ground that did not appear to have had any care for a century or more. It was in a grove of oak trees, so old and large that they had smothered out the underbrush.

The graves were heavily covered in leaves for the most part, but here and there a marker pushed up through the debris. A low stone wall surrounding one small lot had partly fallen down. Within the enclosure a small stone showed clearly above the leaves. I did a double take when I read what was written on it:

Buried here is Elizabeth Ellen James,
who died July 5, 1879, in the 70th year of her age.
She was married nine times
but never found the happiness she sought.

Too many years had passed. I knew that inquiry in the neighborhood would be in vain.

NOT WHAT HE SOUGHT

Recent visitors to an old cemetery in Floyd County, Virginia, told me that an epitaph I had copied some 40 years earlier is now completely illegible:

William Shakespeare Cleek, 1870-1901
Thou shalt not covet thy neighbor's wife,
But poor Bill Cleek did.
He sought life's joyous cup,
But found his grave instead.

A little research in the neighborhood revealed that an irate husband had shot not only Bill, but his own wife as well. She survived and soon divorced her husband and married Henry Cleek, an older brother of Bill's. She apparently was determined to have a Cleek!

TELLING IT LIKE IT IS

In south central Virginia I found a nice, black granite monument (rather expensive, I would say) set among what appears to have been a large family—brothers, sisters, parents, uncles, aunts, and perhaps grandparents. What makes the monument outstanding is the frank statement inscribed upon it:

In fond memory of "Black" Bill Strum
July 12, 1879 – July 13, 1939
Though never married, he was the father of
seventeen children, all now living,
and who now deeply mourn his passing.
Erected by his devoted children – 1939

Though most of the surviving Strums had moved elsewhere, I met a relative who informed me that Black Bill, a Caucasian, received his nickname because of his dark complexion. Bill was a mason skilled with both brick and stone, and his relative pointed out several of his buildings. He also said that one woman gave birth to ten of his children and that he had taken good care of all his illegitimate offspring. As the marker claims, they were all quite fond of him.

Lots of interesting things have happened in this old world!

TEMPTATION

In north central North Carolina, not far from where lived the "hero" of the previous story, I came across another marker that tells it like it is. I could not help but wonder who had erected such a frank stone:

Sacred to the memory of Rev. John Z. Fall
Born May 8, 1823
Died May 30, 1903
Here lies the body of preacher Johnny Fall,
Who really wasn't much preacher at all.
For when an Eve offered an apple,
Johnny would always fall.

PROLIFIC MOTHER

In the uplands of northwestern South Carolina I ran across a small, supposedly public cemetery that didn't appear to have had a burial in 50 or more years. Young pines have sprouted up all over, portending that eventually it will turn into a pine grove.

Several wood grave markers are fast decaying. Crude mountain stones mark other graves. One modest store-bought marker bears the name of Celia Hunsucker, who was born in 1840 and died in 1894 at the age of 54. Her grave is sort of to itself, in a back corner of the burial ground. No husband lies by her side, and apparently none of her many children are buried there. The verse on her marker tells of her notable accomplishment:

> Some mothers have many children,
> Some have none,
> But here lies the mother of twenty-one.

Was her large family due to extra strong passions? I doubt it. More than likely, she bore them because of a sense of drab duty. (I'm just thinking out loud now!)

I could not find another Hunsucker in the entire community, and no one could enlighten me on the matter. Few even knew of the little abandoned cemetery.

The Unusual

Throughout the Southland are many markers with inscriptions that, while not outright humorous, are so different, so unusual, that they cannot be ignored. Several examples follow.

LONG WIDOWHOOD

In Sabine Parish, Louisiana, I located a marker that told of the lengthy widowhood of Sarah Sabrina Long. She died at the age of 97, on June 5, 1899. Below her name and dates is a bit of unusual information:

> She was married three months and was a widow 79 years.

I learned that her three months of marriage produced one son, whose descendants lived in or around Houston, Texas.

CHERISHED HOPE

In Iberville Parish, Louisiana, lived a rich gambler named Henry Droke. He indeed once was wealthy, but when he died, his brothers had to pay his funeral and burial expenses. And they went a little further and erected him a substantial tombstone, which some say is now lost in the dense growth of a long-abandoned plantation. But a few years ago I copied the inscription and now share it with you:

> Here is buried poor Henry Droke,
> Who long was very rich,
> But died very broke,
> We hope that in the better land,
> He will be very rich again.

LETHAL GHOST

The overgrown, fenceless family cemetery in Pickens County, South Carolina, is a spooky looking place even in daytime. I learned that it fell victim to endless neglect when the family moved away from the area. A magnolia and two large holly trees shut out all sunlight, and the shade has pretty much left the ground free from undergrowth. The few store-bought stones are stained and partly covered with moss.

One of the markers bears an inscription that caused me to feel I had a story, if I could locate an informer. The man who had told me of the site knew nothing further. He had stumbled upon the long deserted cemetery when hunting, and the strange epitaph on one of the well-stained stones had impressed him:

> Hannah Wilson
> August 19, 1870
> May 20, 1926
> She was scared to death
> by a ghost that wasn't real.

The remote cemetery lay on a farm that appeared long abandoned, and my search for further information proved difficult. I could find no one named Wilson in the vicinity. Finally someone directed me to an older man who lived in the town of Sunset and supposedly knew about everything that had ever happened in the county.

He had only a vague recollection of "hearing tell" of something like that. But he remembered that a country doctor had served the community for years. He was dead, but he had a daughter still living in Spartanburg, 60 miles away. He said she was rather old but might remember something about such an unusual incident.

As it happened, I would be going through Spartanburg the next day on my way to Hudson, North Carolina. I found the lady listed in the telephone directory and called her. In a little while she ushered me into the sitting room of her commodious home.

Gracious and kind, she exhibited a sincere desire to help. Yes, she had been reared in Pickens County, her father had been the doctor for that portion of that county, and she did remember the incident!

"The Wilsons moved in there from North Carolina," she began. "They owned no land, but for years they lived on my father's older brother's place as tenants. This was about two, maybe two and a half miles from where we lived.

"Hannah Wilson was an old-maid sister of the father of the family. She lived with them. I can remember her very well. She was rather nervous—excitable, I would say—and I have heard said that she was mortally afraid of what folks in that area called hants. And I well remember that night, just after dark as I recollect, when one of the teenaged Wilson boys came running for Dad. He was very excited and could scarcely blurt out that his aunt Hannah had passed out at the milk gap [a small portion of the barnyard where milking was done] and couldn't be revived. Dad later told that they had drawn cold well water and poured all over her in a vain attempt to bring her to.

"The day before that happened, her brother's oldest son—I think his name was Hassell—had died of typhoid fever. There was an old family cemetery up on the hill just back of the barnyard, and they buried him there that late afternoon before this happened. It was getting very late when everything was over up there, almost dusky dark I think, when the family came back down to the house.

"Some of the others went about various chores while Hannah and one of the Wilson girls went to do the milking. I guess it was getting pretty dark by then. The niece later said that a neighbor man who had been at the burying had gone on around the hill to see a family that lived there, and was returning home. His path was right through the pasture by the milking place. Hannah heard him whistling, looked up, and could barely see his tall form as he came walking closer. She screamed out, 'It's Hassell—he's come back from the dead.' And then she just fell backward off that stool; they thought she'd fainted, but she was dead. Well, that man was extra tall, like Hassell, and Hassell did go about the place whistling a lot. So I suppose that neighbor could have easily been mistaken for the dead nephew.

"I recollect seeing Dad ride off on his big horse with the Wilson boy behind him. Though he got there just as quickly as he could, nothing could be done. Hannah was long dead by then. She was buried up there in that old family cemetery. The Wilsons soon left there—moved to Tennessee, I think. My uncle soon sold the place. I hear that it's all grown up now."

Indeed it is all grown up. But a stone still marks the grave of a woman who was scared to death by a ghost that wasn't real.

SHE STAYED CLOSE TO HOME

Deep in the mountains of Western North Carolina sits an old house, made of wide hewed logs, on a homestead that has served the Allen family since the early 1800s. A family cemetery just back of a garden beside the house contains burials from all those generations, including one whose gravestone bears a lengthy inscription telling of the unusual life of one of the first-generation Allens:

Lucretia D. Allen
Born July 17, 1818 – Died July 17, 1899

She spent all her 81 years in the house in which she was born, and was never over 11 miles from home. She did not spend one night away from the house of her birth. She never once had a doctor, and never had a dose of medicine. She died peacefully in the same bed, and in the same room where she was born, on her birthday and at the same hour of her birth. She was never married but helped to raise 22 of her widowed brothers' and sisters' children. She was a member of the Holly Grove Baptist Church and only missed three Sundays in 75 years, those being the three Sundays before she died. This monument erected by 22 of her grateful nieces and nephews, 1900.

THEY HAD TO BE NICKNAMED

A few miles from where Lucretia Allen lived her remarkable life, six men, all named John Adams, are buried in an old mountain cemetery. They all lived at about the same time and were cousins of some degree. In life they had to be nicknamed in order to tell of whom one was speaking. That situation existed in a lot of mountain communities.

Their nicknames all begin with *F*, and most are self-explanatory. With one notable exception, each man's nickname is inscribed on his tombstone for easy identification.

"Fighting" John Adams had a large family who all lived nearby. According to informants, he was always ready to fight at the drop of a hat, and he seemed to enjoy it. Once a fight ended, he would try to be friends with his opponent, often successfully. But, alas, his final rival—a cousin, but not another John Adams—fatally stabbed him.

"Fancy" John Adams, though not wealthy, tried to spruce up far beyond his means. He even wore a bow tie when plowing his fields. At any neighborhood gathering, he managed somehow to be the best-dressed person there. Because his ways were unusual in the mountains, he was not well liked, even by his numerous Adams cousins. And his wife apparently did not like him either; she left him after two years of marriage and returned to her family on the Yadkin River. He had no immediate family and spent the rest of his years as a bachelor. His is a lone grave in a back corner of the cemetery.

"Fiddling" John Adams was just that; he fiddled every chance he got. He learned his art as a child, an old-timer told me, adding that "his fiddlin' could've made a preacher dance." Traveling near and far to play his fiddle, he sometimes lost a crop, and because of his frequent absences, his wife and twelve children practically had to run the farm. He suddenly died while fiddling for a dance on Laurel Branch.

Little explanation is needed for "Fat" John Adams. He ate like a hog, and his body responded accordingly. His wife was fat, as well, and all their children grew large as they became older. He could hardly find store-bought clothes that fit, and eventually his clothing all had to be home-made. No one knew how much he weighed, but guesses ran up to 400 pounds. His homemade casket, one lady told me, was "wide as a wagon bed." His grave also had to be dug extra wide, and additional men were needed to "rope him down" into the ground. Even his large homemade tombstone is on the "fat" order.

"Feisty" John Adams, a bachelor, lived up to his nickname. He "just feisted about," one informant told me, and would never settle down. Some said he was "a bit touched in the head." He preferred the company of children and played childish games with them as long as he could during his 87 years. He lived with an older brother, until that brother died. Then he took up residence with a younger brother, who was known as "Stiller" Jim Adams because he operated an illicit still. Feisty John died at his younger brother's home and was buried in the family row.

Now, there is another John Adams in that cemetery who also had a nickname beginning with *F*, but the word is not mentioned or discussed in mixed company, nor did it appear on his tombstone. Deferring to those who might be shocked, I will not write it here, but it was quite a joke among the more worldly men in the community.

A Genealogical Puzzle

Just back of the orchard on a farm in the mountains of western Virginia is a little family cemetery on a pleasant tree-shaded knoll. A white Georgia marble grave marker shaped like an obelisk bears a real genealogical puzzle:

> Here resting in the hope of a better home above
> is Miranda Collins Jenkins,
> who was born April 6, 1850,
> and departed this life October 3, 1929.
> She married three Jenkins in a row,
> John Simerly Jenkins,
> his son, Wilton James Jenkins,
> and his son, Robert Williams Jenkins,
> father, son and grandson in descending order.
> She bore children by all three.
> Now tell me, you who pass by, what relation are the children?

A bit of inquiry turned up the information that in 1866, just before her 16th birthday, Miranda married John, who was around 45 years old. They had three children before his death seven years later. She then married John's son, Wilton, a 30-year-old widower with a 10-year-old son named Robert. Together they had four children before Wilton died some 10 years later. Miranda then married her stepson, whom she had helped raise.

Two years earlier, Robert had married a girl who was only 14. Her parents had the marriage annulled—but not soon enough. A child was born to them. The girl eloped again a year or so later, leaving the child with her widowed mother. After Miranda and Robert married, the widowed mother died, so they took and raised the baby in their home.

Though Miranda was 33 and her last husband 20 when they married, the marriage is said to have been near ideal. They had five children.

Now, if things were not complicated enough, after Miranda died, Robert, then in his 60s, married her niece, who was about 30, and they had five more children. And the puzzle doesn't end there. An old-timer in the area, a younger first cousin of the first husband, John, revealed what may have been a long-kept family secret.

"That there tombstone don't tell it all," he said with a mischievous twinkle in his eye. "Miranda already had a young'un when she married Cousin John. She got bigged by Uncle Marion Jenkins when she's 'bout 14, I reckon. Marion were a brother to my pap and Cousin John's pap. He was an old widder man when that happened, 'bout 60 year old, I think. Uncle Marion allus [always] was kinda roguish—even when he's married—and Pap allus said that Miranda was takin' to the bresh [brush] with boys by the time she was 13. Now, I reckon Cousin John was a first cousin of his stepson, and they's lots of other ways that bunch is mixed up."

Yes, there are lots of other ways this family is mixed up—ways that I have never been able to figure out. Can you?

A Very Private Person

In about as a remote a place as one can find in northwestern Arkansas is the final resting place of Adam Cicero Moses Freeman. Surrounded by dense woods, his solitary grave at the head of a rough, bluff-sided hollow, and near the top of a rather high mountain, is now a part of the the Ozark National Forest.

Many years after his death, a nephew, who made a great deal of money as a moonshiner, erected the marble monument that now marks his grave. That nephew knew his uncle well and had the marker inscribed accordingly:

Adam Cicero Moses Freeman
1833 – 1899

He was buried in this lonely place at his request.
He hated people in life, and he didn't want to be near
them in death. He didn't want to go to heaven or hell
because he feared they might be overcrowded.
Stranger don't tarry long at this site. He wants to be alone.

From mountain lore oft repeated in the locality, I learned that his ghost lurked in the nearby woods and would chase anyone who stood long near his grave. A few hunters reported seeing strange lights and hearing mournful sounds if they ventured too near at night.

He had married a first cousin when young, and a few months later she died. (The young bride is buried in a community cemetery perhaps two miles from her husband's grave.) After her death, he became a hermit. More or less living off the land, he took up residence in an old abandoned barn in the valley and roamed the woods day and night, never venturing out into civilization.

Near the end of his life, after he was found sick and helpless near his "humble home," he lived with a brother (father of the man who erected the monument) and left instructions for his burial. So today he sleeps in that lonely grave, under a blanket of fallen leaves of many autumns past. Likely many years pass between the appearances of visitors to the site.

Placing a Curse

In central Mississippi I discovered one of those rare tombstone inscriptions that show the venomous feelings of the person who saw to the erection of the marker. The epitaph also includes another rarity, the manner of death of the deceased:

> To the memory of Thomas Keeling,
> who on December 10, 1904 fell into a ditch
> while being chased by a mean dog
> and there broke his neck.
> Cursed be that dog and his owner.

I could find no further details of the tragic accident.

He Ought to Have Known Better

Perhaps 50 miles west of Nashville, Tennessee, is a simple grave marker bearing an unusual epitaph that ends with a judgmental statement:

> Sacred to the memory of my husband,
> Madison B. Keller,
> who was born on February 12, 1890,
> and died during the summer of 1919.
> His death came by his eating too many wild cherries,
> and drinking a quart of buttermilk with them.
> He ought to have known better.

To say the least, the man had a strange appetite. Would you like cherries and buttermilk together? I also wonder if the wife had forgotten the date of her husband's demise.

Sweet Sleep at Last

In Escambia County, Alabama, and "pert nigh on the Florida line," as my informant of long ago expressed it, used to be a marker that told of Sampson Cornett, an early settler to the county, who was born in 1776 and died in 1870. His epitaph told the story of his strange manner of life:

> Sampson Cornett is sleeping at last!
> He seldom slept over one hour per night,
> yet was healthy, energetic, accomplished much.
> He remained very active until his death at the age of 94.
> He now will sleep a long time.
> May his awakening be to everlasting life.

Take heed, you who sleep your life away!

Whole Lot of Lying

Until embarrassed descendants had it taken down and replaced with a standard tombstone (and standard inscription), there was a grave marker in Hamilton County, Florida, erected over the grave of a lawyer who seemed to have a compulsion to tell it like it was! After his name and dates appeared a rather frank and revealing epitaph:

> He lied much in life until death ended his
> long career of lying for a living, but now, at last he
> is lying here, and will be lying for a long time.

He on the Left, She on the Right

While living briefly in Breathitt County, Kentucky, several years ago, I knew a delightful old couple, and I often think of them even to this day. The Mortons were delightful as individuals, that is. As a couple at home, their lives must have been far different.

I well remember that their large, two-story home, filled with fine antique furniture, was the most impressive in the village. Oftentimes I passed down the road in front of their home and was likely to see them on the fancy portico that graced the front of their charming old house. They seemed so at peace. Always he sat on the far left side of the portico, while she sat on the far right.

I did hear rumors about them, though. A neighbor lady said that Mrs.

Morton cooked Mr. Morton's food, set it on the dining table, then retired to the kitchen and ate alone. I wondered much about it but did not make further inquiry.

The last time I saw the Mortons, they were taking advantage of a sunny, balmy fall day by sitting quietly on that fancy portico, she on the right, as usual, and he on the left. Just how quietly they sat, I was yet to learn.

A year and a half later, I returned to the community for a brief stay. The dear old couple had both died and had been buried side by side in the family cemetery along the top of a ridge overlooking their homeplace.

"You just ought to go up there and see what that strange son of theirs had put on that marker," the postmaster told me.

I climbed up the ridge to where they were buried, and found that they had a substantial, gray granite marker. Below the vital data was the revealing epitaph:

Isaac Winfield Morton	Lula Smith Morton
May 19, 1863	September 24, 1861
August 2, 1957	October 22, 1957

They were married 72 years, but never spoke to one another for the last 61 of those years. Praise God that there is no marriage in Heaven!

STILL A REBEL

In those seemingly endless pine flats in southeastern Georgia I found an emphatic declaration on a marker for an ex-Confederate soldier, who apparently never ceased being a rebel:

He was a rebel of 1861-65,
and remained a rebel all his life,
and died a rebel.
Alone he killed thirteen Federals
in a skirmish near this place,
and wished it could have been thirteen thousand.
He lived in hopes that his grandsons
would get to fight those infernal Yankees again.

RELIEF AT LAST

In Sumter County, South Carolina, I found a fading inscription on the marker at the grave of Jennie Crawford, who was born in 1831 and died in 1909. She apparently died during a sneezing bout that was of unusual duration. Her epitaph tells the story:

> For five weeks she sneezed fast,
> No relief could she find,
> But relief did come at last,
> When she left this world behind.

I spent only one day and night in the county, so I did not have time to make further inquiry.

Was There No Peace in This Life?

Some epitaphs can create a question in the mind of the viewer, such as this one found on a marker in Johnston County, North Carolina:

> Here lies side-by-side
> Arthur Peavler and his wife,
> Cynthia Kernan Peaveler,
> who were married 64 years.
> Now they have peace at last.

Did they not have peace during their 64 years of marriage? We wonder!

Sad Fate

In central Virginia is a small family burial ground high on a windswept hill. From the several elaborate monuments in the little plot, I came to the conclusion that a rather prosperous family rests here. Among those fine monuments is a plain one that tells a melancholy story:

> Here lies all that was mortal of Sarah Ellen Long-Harmon
> who was born in 1850, and died in 1913.
> In her younger years she was a brilliant and
> highly intelligent schoolteacher.
> But, alas, she spent the last 41 years of her life
> in the Western State Hospital at Staunton, Virginia,
> all brought about by the waywardness of
> her erring and unfaithful husband, Druid Harmon.

The Long descendants who lived in the area at the time of my visit would not share information about the unfortunate lot of their lamented family member. But I did learn that her "erring" husband had remarried a few years after her admission to the mental hospital in Staunton, and he had moved to North Carolina and reared a large family.

OUTSTANDING ACCOMPLISHMENT

In Marengo County, Alabama, is a small overgrown graveyard on what I suppose was a former plantation divided into smaller tracts of land. I strongly suspect that it was a slave cemetery that may have been later used by free blacks. Out of perhaps 25 graves, only three are marked, including an interesting inscription on a store-bought gravestone:

Aunt Hannah Reed, who died in 1899, aged 99,
who had not a tooth in her head for 60 years of her long life,
yet she ate without trouble, and stayed fat until her dying day.

Aunt Hannah likely was an ex-slave who had been freed at the close of the Civil War.

HOPES TO TAKE A FLYING TRIP

This man could not have flown in an airplane, because he died before such was invented. Nevertheless, he expressed a hope of flying. Over his grave in Cheatham County, Tennessee, is a face-up style marker bearing this epitaph:

I died on Sunday,
Was buried on Monday,
Don't know the day I shall arise,
But hope to fly off to the skies.

HE DIED TRYING

In Randolph or Lawrence County, Arkansas—my notes do not say, and I have forgotten—I found a white marble, rounded-top marker at the grave of Macon "Buck" Priddy, who was born in Tennessee in 1820 and died in Arkansas in 1883. His epitaph tells a complete, albeit short, story:

He was great he was good,
But he died while chopping wood.
A full rick he would make it,
But his heart just couldn't take it.
The sun shone hot, but he chopped on,
The rick's still short—the chopper's gone.

Self Excusers Beware

In eastern Texas I found an obelisk tombstone that bears a mini sermon. Whoever erected it took the opportunity to warn against the practice of carrying on secular activities on Sunday instead of attending church. The epitaph tells of a poor young man who was killed at the age of 26:

Here is buried Jimmy Doggett
who was killed by a bull when crossing the
pasture of Richard Harmon on his way to fish
on Sunday, July 5, 1896, at about 11:30 A.M.
He ought to have been in church,
and this would not have happened.
Take warning, you who would
excuse yourselves from church services.

The Final Crossing

In the beautiful New River Valley of southwestern Virginia I found a rather impressive, tall, white marble monument with an unusual inscription:

Here awaiting the great resurrection morning is
J. Franklin Reddell
born May 12, 1850
and drowned April 17, 1887
when he tried to cross New River
during a heavy flood time.
He ought not to have tried it.
If he had stayed where he ought to have stayed,
he would not be where he now is.

Well, I suppose that is a reasonable conclusion!

He Came to the Truth

In Phillips County, Arkansas, on the grave marker of an affluent planter is inscribed a short statement of profound truth:

I was rich but now wealth doesn't matter.

Blessed Hope

Deep in the most mountainous section of southeastern Kentucky is a child-sized monument, which usually, but not always, indicates a poor family. On it is a personalized verse, likely composed by the bereaved husband:

> Here lies the wife of Hiriam Brown,
> It sure was sad when she went down.
> But coming up will happy be,
> I hope I am around to see!

SHORT LIFE EXPLAINED

In the same section of Kentucky as mentioned above is another small marker over the grave of one who died at age 29. The one-line epitaph explains his short life:

> James Henry Everett
> 1880-1909
> He got drunk one time too many.

An old-timer in the neighborhood told me that this unfortunate young man went to a dance, where he became drunk. He took a mountain trail on his way home, fell over a bluff, and broke his neck.

A FRANK DESCRIPTION

In Jackson Parish, Louisiana, is a crude marker that bears a frank apprisal of the physical attributes of Louise Brombeck, who was born in 1871 and died in 1913. I could find no one in the area who could give me further light on the matter, except for a clue given by an elderly lady: "I think them Brombecks left here years ago and moved somewhere way out in Texas." Well, perhaps the stone tells enough:

> She was harelipped, had faded red hair, a big crooked nose, big buck teeth, was cross-eyed and weighed close to three hundred pounds, yet she managed to marry two of the most handsome men in this Parish.

I could not help but wonder who ordered the inscription on her stone.

FROM BLINDNESS TO VISION

One of the first strange epitaphs I found was in a family burial ground in Haywood County, Tennessee, located on a former farm that had been cut up into many small tracts. The stone was then leaning backward, so if it has since fallen, perhaps the inscribed side is face upward. It memorialized Almon St. John, who was born in 1822 in Buncombe County, North Carolina, and died in 1892. Below his name and dates it reads:

> He was born blind, and never saw a thing in this world,
> but now sees wondrous things in Heaven.

Following the inscription is a quotation from "Amazing Grace," an old hymn often sung throughout the Southland: "I once was blind but now I see."

DEAF MUTE

On a cedar-covered knoll in Bosque County, Texas, is an old, abandoned cemetery where cows roamed freely at the time of my visit. One stone, already knocked down by the roving cattle, bears an inscription making it clear that the person memorialized was a deaf mute:

> Poor Jim Lakin,
> Was the strangest man around.
> He couldn't hear it thunder,
> And couldn't make a sound!

AT LEAST A MUTE

Several hundred miles east of Bosque County, Texas, in Limestone County, Alabama, I found another marker memorializing one who at least was a mute:

> Here sleeps Surilda Dowdy,
> Who in her life never said howdy.
> It's very true, many can recall,
> That she could not say any word at all.

Dates on her stone show that she died in 1911 at the age of 89.

THE RHYMING FAMILY

In the Piedmont of North Carolina is a large farm, still productive and home to a family not related to the original owners, the Cranfields. The current residents diligently keep the little family cemetery back of the peach orchard in good condition. Several flowering bushes decorate the fencerows along the graveyard. The stones there are modest but tasteful, all still legible and upright. One row of graves has only one marker, but it contains all the vital information, including a revealing epitaph:

> Here in a row rests the five Cranfield sisters,
> Ollie, Holly, Molly, Nollie, and Dolly,
> none of whom ever married.
> They all slept in the same room in the family home
> from girlhood to old age—even to the time of their deaths.
> Ollie was the cook, Holly was the housekeeper,
> Molly and Nollie taught at the local school,
> and Dolly was the family seamstress.
> They had four brothers, John, Don, Ron, and Lon,
> none of whom are buried here.

The dates reveal that the last survivor of the group, Molly, had the longest life, dying at the age of 98. The nearby family home is still in a good state of repair. Children of the present owners occupy the east upstairs room that was long inhabited by the five sisters.

AFRAID OF RAZORS?

In Lauderdale County, Mississippi, is buried Joshua Starnes, born in Georgia in 1832, and died in 1895. His epitaph tells of an unusual aspect of his life:

> In all his life he never did shave,
> Now he lies, long beard and all,
> In this lonely grave.

Considering the bare, long-blade style razors used in those days, I venture that he might have been afraid of those potentially lethal "weapons."

AFRAID OF SCISSORS?

Hundreds of miles to the northeast of Lauderdale County, Mississippi, is Camden County, North Carolina. Perhaps the counterpart of Joshua Starnes is buried there. A marker to George Phillips's grave in the central part of that county states:

> He never had a haircut in all his long life.
> At his death, aged 87, it reached almost to his waist.

Was he as afraid of scissors as Joshua Starnes was of razors?

HE TRIED TO SAVE BUT LOST

In Ottawa County, in the northeast corner of Oklahoma, I found a marker that told of the sad fate of Willie Senter. The inscription indicated that evidently he was a thrifty man who died trying to extend the life of his longhandles:

> Here sleeps poor Willie Senter,
> Who usually wore longies all the winter.
> He shed them early some wear to save,
> And that brought him to the grave.

I have since learned that the marker no longer exists.

YOUNG MURDERER

The Cumberland Mountain range between Knoxville and Nashville, Tennessee, is not the most likely place in the South to find strange epitaphs. Indeed, most gravestone inscriptions in the area are of the religious, sentimental type. But in an overgrown, hillside cemetery in a deep valley in that mountain range, I found a stone that intrigued me:

> Asleep in Jesus is Prof. Manley Owens,
> who was born in Emanuel County, Georgia, July 12, 1866,
> and was murdered at Beech Springs School, August 20, 1901,
> by Delton Stevens, one of his thirteen-year-old pupils.

Of course, I lost no time in seeking out the story. And I had a clue to start on. I had seen the name Claud Stevens in faint, barely readable lettering on a mailbox that I passed when I had driven to the cemetery. I drove back down the rough, dusty road to the battered mailbox. Near it was a narrow primitive road, barely more than a trail, that wound up and over a low ridge.

I followed that road, filled with the sometimes-strong feeling that often comes to me when I am near the source of much-desired information. Just over the ridge stood a crude, hill-country house with a long, low front porch. On the shady end of the porch sat a gnarled, gray-haired man, who proved to be Claud Stevens. I soon learned that he was a first cousin to Delton Stevens, who had murdered Prof. Owens. How lucky could I get!

When I made my query, he eagerly replied: "Why, shore, I can tell ye all about that. Delton Stevens—we called him Delt—was my first cousin, my uncle Tom's boy. And I was in the first batch of scholars that come that morning and found teacher Owens shot dead. He was a-layin' all bloody in the floor ahind his teachin' table. Ye see, that table was set near the back winder. Jist only had room for his cheer ahind it. Delt had slipped up to that winder and shot him in the back of his head as he was readin' a book, a-gettin' ready fer teachin' that day. I allus [always] wondered if he knowed what had hit him.

"Owens come in here from somers [somewhere] in Georgia—don't recollect just where it was. Now he got taken on to teach two terms at old Beech Springs. That schoolhouse were at the springs jist above the graveyard ye was in. No sign of hit now, 'cept old rocks where the steps was.

"Ye see, the day afore that happent, that teacher had whupped the tar outen Delt. Cousin Delt were a powerful stubborn boy, and was allus into meanness. Now, afterwards, Delt bragged that he'd kill that teacher shore. We didn't mind him much—jist thought he'd git over his mad spell.

"Well, next mornin', whilst Uncle Tom and Aunt Fannie—that were Uncle Tom's wife—were out milkin', he got Uncle Tom's big pistol—it were a .45, I thank—and hurried off to the schoolhouse by a back way. He knowed Owens allus got there long afore any of us scholars. Tracks showed he had come across the field ahind that schoolhouse and up to that winder, and there he done hit.

"Now, iffen you'da looked there under that old holly tree in the back corner of that graveyard, you'da found Delt's grave. Aunt Fannie set that tree soon after Delt died. Reckon he died the same day he shot the teacher.

"He just seemed to disappear that day after he shot Owens. But 'bout a week later his body was found where hit had warshed up on a rock bar jist below the long hole over here in the creek. Ah reckon he had been hightailin' hit, but must have tried to cross there about the long hole. Would had to swum if he tried the long hole, fer hit's powerful deep. The water was sort of on a rise that day—had rained hard back up on the head. So I guess hit overcome him, and he drownded plumb dead. Uncle Tom's pistol was never found. If Delt had hit with him, I guess hit's still in the long hole.

"Now, he's got a sister still a-livin'. She lives at the end of that road about a mile past the graveyard. But won't do no good to see her, fer she won't talk about it a-tall."

I didn't go see her; I had heard enough!

POLITICS IN STONE

In my extensive travels throughout the South I have found a few markers bearing inscriptions clearly showing that the deceased very much wanted to put in a last word for his political party, its beliefs, and its practices. You may just about bet that those persons memorialized by these markers were rabid party loyalists. Far down in southern Georgia, in an area where one would not have expected to find a Republican—at least in the early twentieth century—I found a rather elaborate, white marble monument bearing a definitely political message:

Albert Thomas McShane

April 20, 1851
August 16, 1940

There rests here one who thanks God
that he never in his long life voted for a Democrat
and urges all who view this stone to follow his example.

No Doubt About It
On a ridge above an eastern Kentucky mining town, a plain marble tombstone bears a short but emphatic statement:

James M. Blair
1864-1939
A DEMOCRAT

He Had Repented and Changed
Far out in a pasture in Lawrence County, Tennessee, is a lone grave over which cattle grazed at the time of my visit. (The fence that had once protected it had been knocked down.) The marker had fallen or been pushed down, but the face side was up, so I could read the inscription:

James Lemuel Barr
Born July 5, 1839
Died January 2, 1914

Here sleeps one who long ago repented
of having voted for Samuel J. Tilden,
and has voted straight Democrat ever after.

He Wanted the World to Know
In the Big Sandy River country of eastern Kentucky, a large public

cemetery sprawls across a low ridge that overlooks that great river valley. Without doubt, the most unique epitaph in that cemetery is found on an impressive monument of one who wanted the world to know his political affiliation:

Robert B. Cummings
Born February 11, 1870
Died September 12, 1931

Here rests one who wants the world to know
that he was born a Republican,
he lived a Republican,
and he died a Republican.

Thanks be to God!

HE LOVED HIS PARTY

In a tiny cemetery (perhaps a family burying ground) in Desoto County, Florida, is buried a man whose marker leaves no doubt as to his love for his political party:

JAMES B. BURNS
1887-1927

He joined the Socialist party in 1920.
He loved that party, and wishes that he could have
lived longer to have supported and promoted the
Socialist, the only good party in America.

I found six more Burns markers in the cemetery, but there was no indication whether or not they were Socialist.

UNUSUAL CAUSE OF DEATH

In McCreary County, Kentucky, I found one of those rare inscriptions telling the manner of death:

Here lies Stephen Dees,
Who while plowing,
Was attacked by bees.
Too many bees, too many stings,
Now he hears the angels sing!

The only other place I have encountered the name Dees was in Boone County, Arkansas.

PUZZLING DATE

In Charlotte, North Carolina, is a very old burying ground that has a marker showing a man's death date as February 30th. I wonder what kind of calendar was used?

CLOSING THOUGHTS

Rarely is an epitaph of any kind inscribed on a marker today. I think this is highly regrettable, and hope that unusual epitaphs may again come into general usage. Meanwhile, let us make an effort to preserve those that do exist. Time and the elements are slowly erasing many of them, and speed in their preservation is imperative. Many of those included here, barely legible when I came across them, may now be completely faded out.

I do not presume to have found every strange or humorous epitaph in Dixie. Far from it. Therefore, I urge all my readers to assist me in my search for more. I am sure there are many out there, and I would like to know about them. If enough are found, I possibly could use them in a future publication. Your help in this quest will be much appreciated.

Unholy LANGUAGE

The stories in this chapter tell of Christians who either forgot where they were, let habit overcome restraint, or yielded to the pressure of an unusual situation by ripping out "bad" words. And those words frequently marked such persons as hypocrites or backsliders before their hearers. One little transgression often was considered sufficient grounds for dismissal from the congregation, and several whose tales are included were promptly excommunicated from their churches because of their language. In many cases, the offender did not have to actually be using the name of the Deity in vain (technical swearing); a simple "damn" might be enough for the ultimate church action.

When I worked as a clerk in a store at Lake Worth, Florida, in Palm Beach County, one of my coworkers was a young lady whose strong Christian profession was well-known. She faithfully attended and supported her church, which taught entire sanctification, a belief that Christians may experience a second work of grace by which they are entirely freed from sinful inclinations. She also had a beautiful singing voice and was sometimes called upon to sing solos for the congregation.

One afternoon she became extremely irritated by something that happened during the course of her duties at work, and she spit forth a four-letter word. Not swearing, mind you, just a word considered "ugly" by those concerned about such things.

Immediately, an older clerk, who was not very religious, pointed an accusing finger at her and said, "You've done backslid; you've said a bad word!"

Many persons who profess the righteous life use bad language occasionally, but only before a select audience. That is, they practice doing as the Romans when in Rome. But it can be risky, because there often is a "Roman" who will go and tell.

Once, a man being tried by a church for swearing said, "No, I don't think anybody in this church heard me cussing, because I'm always careful never to cuss in public."

Some professors of religion talk as they please without regard to what others (and presumably the church) may think. And there are many churches that do not care what language their members may use. But virtually all the churches mentioned in this chapter did care, and usually in a very pronounced manner.

However, with much forgiveness and understanding, what was once deadly serious for church courts years ago has now become humorous to most of us.

STRANGE PRAYER

A few miles northwest of Bristol, Tennessee/Virginia, just off the Gate City Highway, stands Union Hope, a picturesque little country church on a low knoll between the forks of a short hollow. Erected in the late 1800s of hand-hewn logs, it was later weatherboarded and painted white. At first used by two or three denominations, it was eventually made into a Bible Presbyterian church, and is now the only congregation of that denomination in the locality.

I have been told that the building sits so near (possibly astride) the Washington County/Scott County line, that no one knows which county it is in. I also learned that when work was being done on the building during a cold, snowy time, a young workman took pneumonia and died. A while later his ghost began to appear on the church grounds and sometimes in the building. But that is another story.

About 1910, a long-remembered revival was held in this little country church. The meetings started in late September and continued through most of October. An old man who lived within sight of the church was considered to be one of the most pious Christians in the community. He was often called upon to lead the congregation in prayer, and one night during the great revival, he was asked to do so. As usual, he prayed long and loud, earnestly beseeching the Lord to convert the sinners of the area, especially "those boys and young men who come every night, but instead of coming inside, they just mill around the grounds."

As he prayed, those young fellows were planning a bit of mischief. Right in the middle of his prayer and just as he called out in a loud, quavering voice, "Oh Lord," one of them threw a rock against the front door. The man's startled prayer thus came out, "Oh, Lord, what the hell was that?"

The boys outside had more to laugh about than they had expected. And there were some among those inside who silently shook with laughter throughout the remainder of the service.

The old man, shamed by his slipup, would never again lead that congregation in prayer.

A FIERY REMINDER

Old Mr. Faulkner was a faithful attendant of the Broad Meadow Nazarene Church near Rolling Fork, Mississippi, even though he was near the point of deafness. His wife, several years his junior, more or less did the listening for him, and after their return home, she would explain the sermon of the day. If she needed to communicate with him during the service, she always cupped her hands to his better ear and whispered loudly—so loud that those sitting nearby could hear her.

One Sunday morning the pastor was preaching on hell and its terrible possibilities. His words on *fire* and *burning* caused Mrs. Faulkner to think of something urgent. Quickly she cupped her hands to her husband's ear and whispered to him. He leaned toward her and muttered, "eh." She then repeated her statement a bit louder. It was plain to see that she was on pins and needles and needed to convey her message with the utmost speed. He just leaned closer and mumbled another inquiry as to what she had said. By that time she was up and reaching for her coat and clutching her purse, and again she whispered loudly in his ear.

Up front the preacher paused for breath after making a spirited statement on the horrors of hell. Mr. Faulkner must have caught a word or two of his wife's plea, for during that moment of silence in the pulpit, he loudly mumbled back to her, "Why no, Berthie, we're not going to burn in hellfire, fer we've both done been saved and plumb sanctified."

Mrs. Faulkner's patience had run out. Forgetting where she was for the moment, she loudly called into his ear, "Durn it, I didn't say we was gonna burn in hellfire. I said that I forgot and left the fire on under the beans, and they're gonna burn if we don't get the hell outta here and get home to them!"

BLIND BELLE MASON LOSES HER RELIGION

East of the Sunflower River, in Sunflower County, Mississippi, is a little village called Pentecost. Perhaps the town was well named. In the early days of the Pentecostal movement, many in that part of the state were converted to that faith. It appears the greatest concentration of these newly made Pentecostals was in a rural area just north and slightly east of the village. The converts in that vicinity largely were free Pentecostals—called free holiness by some—that is, they were not part of any organized denominational body; they formed their own rules of faith and practice.

If anyone, man or woman, felt the urge to preach, he or she, educated or not, simply started preaching—without denominational instruction, approval, license, or ordination. As a consequence, one might hear many strange and "far out" ideas bantered around during lengthy, spirited, and lively sermons.

The principal meeting place for Pentecostals in that region was an old, weather-beaten, never painted two-room schoolhouse situated in a grove of scrub oak trees. Once known as Oak Grove, the building later bore two or three other names. (There had been a dispute in the community over what to call it.)

A wide doorway with a set of folding doors separated the school's two rooms. If the first room became full, the doors could be folded back, thus doubling the space. If a preacher was able to draw a crowd large enough to necessitate using both rooms, he was called a "door opener" preacher, and that gave him a bit of local prestige.

During revivals, which came often during the hot Mississippi summers, it was frequently necessary to fold the doors back. At such times the seats in both rooms were turned so that the crowd could view the open door area, where the preaching and special singing took place. The mourners' bench was also located there, where repentant sinners could "pray through" under the gaze of both rooms.

Each room had an outside door leading to a small front porch. These two doors were left wide open for the little breeze that might flow in, and to let some of the heated air out. (A crowd of people can generate an amazing amount of heat in an enclosed room—winter or summer.) Too, the doors served as an easy exit for those who might wander in and out during the hours-long events.

Rare was the person who stayed put during an entire service. Even the most "holy" of the group most often would find cause to leave for a few minutes. Going in and out was the rule among the "unholy," especially the younger set. Even some of the believers, both young and old, might sneak out now and then for a quick smoke far enough out in the dark to be undetected. (The Pentecostals were hard against smoking.) It was not unusual for a little strong drink to be available near the meeting grounds.

That, too, drew a lot of interest among some of those present. And some of the younger folks sought opportunities to get far from the meeting place to a sizeable brush thicket in the corner of an abandoned field. No further explanation needed.

Water supply during hot, dry summer months was also a problem for the crowds that gathered for the protracted meetings. There was a well near the schoolhouse, but by mid-summer it was usually dry. The yard of a farmhouse perhaps a quarter of a mile away had a good well, from which a big bucket of water was often carried to a table on the west porch, where it soon was eagerly consumed by those lucky enough get hold of the single dipper. Everyone, diseased or not, drank from the same dipper.

One July long ago, a wild-eyed, overzealous, unlearned but earnest Pentecostal preacher from Belzoni, Mississippi, came into the community and soon had a door-opener meeting going. He could draw a big crowd in any kind of weather, a crowd that would not be disappointed if a good lively spiritual show was desired, and few ever went away disappointed. Though the weather was exceedingly hot, overflow crowds filled the old schoolhouse just about all the remainder of that summer. Indeed, the revival went on so long that several persons were saved, backslid, and were saved again before the meeting ended—or so they said.

Folks came in droves from near and far. From both sides of the Sunflower River, from north and south, east and west, they came by every imaginable conveyance available, with many walking several miles to get there. And such a varied crowd it was, from the elderly to babies in arms, and all age levels in between. Some came for a spiritual feast, and others came to "see the show," as was often said; but for whatever reason, they came, much to the delight of that crowd-loving preacher.

There was no piano in the schoolhouse, but the meetings never lacked for music, plenty of it and plenty loud. From all over the region, musicians came bringing their guitars, banjos, mandolins, and, yes, even a fiddle or two. All these players spent several minutes before each service tuning their instruments together.

Each day's service began with lots of music and spirited singing. There was much foot stomping and hand clapping, and usually, before three songs were rendered, several of the congregation would be dancing in the aisles, dripping sweat, but dancing right on. Everyone else would be perspiring from the heat, though perhaps to a lesser degree. Most of them were used to sweltering in sweat as they labored on the nearby farms anyway, so it made little difference.

Much praying by all who desired to pray out loud—all at the same time—followed the singing. A hundred people or so, each trying to out-holler the other in a low-ceiling building, can create a roar and din that is unimaginable unless you have heard such. And usually during prayer time, several got "struck by the power," which was certain to bring on much shouting, jumping, dancing, and perhaps much talking in the "unknown tongue." Generally it took a good thirty minutes to an hour before things quieted down to where the order of the service could proceed.

Next came a time of testifying, wherein anyone who so desired could briefly take the floor and tell of his or her religious experiences. Some of the more zealous used the opportunity to just about preach a long sermon during that time. Again there was likely to be shouting, dancing, and talking in tongues, all interspersed by lively dance-worthy music and singing.

Perhaps by eleven o'clock that night, preaching could start, and what preaching. That evangelist from Belzoni would soon be running up and down the aisles, jumping, waving his arms, kicking, and occasionally leaping over benches. Finally he would give a call for mourners, and he was usually rewarded by several coming forward, casting themselves on the mourners' bench, all the while calling loudly for mercy. If a sinner finally "came through," a new round of shouting and all that went with it would take place.

Many did "get religion" during that long revival. But strangely, it was at the height of the meeting that "Blind" Belle Mason lost hers, or so the Pentecostal believers in that community thought.

Blind Belle was not really blind, but her eyesight was so poor that she appeared to be. Squinting at everything, she had to hold any object near her eyes in order to discern what it was. She was also mentally retarded. And like many retarded folks, she had a talent that was especially pronounced. Though she never had a music lesson in her life, she could expertly play the parlor organs that were in some of the better homes of the area.

Blind Belle lived for a time in the home of Melvin Smith, helping out when his wife was mortally sick. When the wife died, Belle was left without a home. Man and woman living together unmarried was not much tolerated in Mississippi at the time, so Melvin just quickly married her so she could stay on with him with some degree of respectability. He too soon died, but the marriage was of such short duration that Belle reverted to her maiden name.

Belle then moved in with a married sister at Boyer, across the Sunflower River and a bit south of Pentecost. But when big revivals were going on in the country above Pentecost, she would come and stay with her brother, John "Butter" Mason (how he got his nickname I never knew), who lived near the Oak Grove schoolhouse. He was one of the strongest of the Pentecostal believers in the entire county, and he was always pleased to have his sister come and join in the spirited services of his church.

Blind Belle claimed to have religion in the strongest degree. "I'm done plumb saved, sanctified, and filled with the Holy Ghost," she would often shout out in the meetings. One particularly hot night during that big revival meeting, she "took the floor" to testify. In no time, she was running around and around the mourners' bench, jumping high and shouting loud. As she did so, it was plain to see that her underskirt was shaking and sliding downward.

A dog that had been lying peacefully on the porch jumped up, ran over to the door, eyed the situation, then made a lunge for Blind Belle. He grabbed her underskirt and began pulling back, growling all the while. The poor woman felt the pull, heard the growl, and whirled around dragging the animal in a half circle. She saw the animal and froze in fear for a brief instant. (She had been dog bitten six or seven times, so she had developed a morbid fear of any dog—large or small, vicious or gentle—they all represented terror to her.)

In a moment she whirled again and rushed forward. Her shouts turned into screams, and she glanced over her shoulder. Looking back proved her undoing; as she did so, she ran into the mourners' bench and fell headlong over it. At about that instant, the dog yanked the underskirt from her. As the garment briefly unfurled like a wind-tossed flag in the air, its words, though a bit faded from numerous washings, still proclaimed, "One hundred pounds of pure sweet sugar."

With Blind Belle's feet high in the air, the remaining top skirt slid all the way to her waist. Alas, whoever had made that sugar-sack underskirt for her had not made any underpants to go with it. So in such a position of both body and skirt, her modesty was not well served!

Almost immediately she jumped up and gave the dog a hard, swinging kick that sent him somersaulting across the room. She yelled loud and strong, "Go to hell, you damn sonofabitching bastard!" Then seeing that in spite of her kick he still had her underskirt in his mouth and was heading for the door, she then shouted, "Some of you damn backsliders out there on that porch, knock that damned dog's head off. He's gettin' away with the only underskirt I've got!"

John Mason was so put out with the unexpected actions and words of his sister that he ran from the schoolhouse and left for home. Belle (minus her treasured underskirt) took out right behind him.

But the show wasn't over. Old Aunt Bonnie Colton, one of the strongest Pentecostals in all Sunflower County, sprang up, shouted a bit, and called out that she had just had a revelation from the Lord that the dog was devil possessed and had been sent to break up the meeting. Then she further revealed that the Lord had said she should "catch the little devil, put him in a sack, and throw him into the river." Having told her orders, she split out the door and began running about over the schoolyard, trying to find Satan's servant so that the directed execution could be carried out. The God of her revelation did not seem to aid her in a successful capture, however. The dog—underskirt and all—had disappeared into the darkness.

Though Pentecostal meetings continued to be held in that schoolhouse for several more years, neither John "Butter" Mason nor "Blind" Belle ever attended again.

THE UNEXPECTED CONFESSION OF MAYE FALLS

Maye Falls, a slightly beautiful, vivacious, outgoing, and often overly friendly young woman, lived on Long Creek in Perry County, Kentucky. After a notorious girlhood—and that is putting it mildly—she married widower Albert Falls, some twenty years her senior. (The folks at the time used the term *notorious* to describe someone with immoral character.) Seemingly, at least for a while, she settled down to married life. Her companionship, great housekeeping, and superb cooking pleased her rather meek and mild husband. One son was born to them within their first year of marriage.

Near the Falls home was the Long Creek Chapel Church, which Maye began attending regularly with her husband. Indeed she became one of the most faithful attendants and was always ready to help in any of its numerous activities.

Another faithful attendant, though not a member of that church, was Clyde Falls, her husband's first cousin. Clyde's youthful years had been about as notorious as had Maye's, and most folks didn't believe he had greatly reformed.

He had married a cranky, complaining, somewhat corpulent, and frequently sick (at least she pretended to be) woman. Unhappy as their marriage may have been, it produced five or six children of the stair-step variety—children born one soon after the other, thus varying little in height.

As the "Raleigh man" for that region, Clyde sold Raleigh products from house to house. Moderately successful, he often showed more interest in women than just as buyers of what he offered for sale.

He frequently stopped at his cousin Albert's home—Maye was one of his best customers—and, in time, rumors began to circulate that she had more interest in Clyde than simply as a supplier of household products.

Maye, who enjoyed paying visits to neighbors up and down a five-mile stretch of Long Creek, sometimes caught rides to her destinations with Clyde, the peddler. And at times his car had been found parked near wooded areas with no one in sight. Too, Clyde seemed to have been fond of calling on Maye at night, ostensibly to sell Raleigh products, but those calls were usually made when Albert was away from home.

Notwithstanding all this suspicion, Maye continued to be loved by a host of friends and neighbors. She was the type of person one could not help loving, in spite of her character flaws. And perhaps because Clyde supplied much-needed products to the entire creek and beyond, he too remained in the public favor.

One day, a fiery young evangelist came from nearby Hazard to conduct a near month-long revival in the Long Creek Chapel Church. In spite of the bone-chilling weather, the revival waxed hot and exciting, causing large crowds to fill the little church night after night. And, of course, Maye was usually the first to arrive and the last to leave. She never seemed to tire of talking long with friends, neighbors, and even strangers who might have come from far-flung communities to hear the evangelist. And Clyde, too, along with his wife and brood of children, nightly came to the lively meetings.

Maye's husband, as a deacon in that church, always sat in the amen corner, on a short bench at the right side of the pulpit. In front of Albert, in the second row, sat Clyde and his family. Maye preferred the bench across the aisle from Clyde, on the left side. The suspicious folks in the congregation noted that sometimes Maye's attention seemed to wander from the preacher to eye Clyde a bit; "to look longingly at him" is the way one of the worldlier of the local men expressed it.

About halfway through the second week, the evangelist preached long and hard against backsliding. He fell into earnest exhortation near the end of his sermon, begging and pleading for those who had strayed from the Father's safe fold to come back home—and quickly—before it was everlastingly too late. Then he led the greatly moved crowd in singing a haunting invitation hymn, "Lord, I'm Coming Home."

The congregation had hardly made it through the first line, when Maye jumped straight up from her bench, threw her hands high in a gesture of surrender, and screamed out, "Lordy, Lordy! Help me, sweet Jesus! I've been a wandering sheep too long, and now I'm coming home!" Down the aisle she ran and flung herself across the mourners' bench, screaming and begging for mercy.

A half dozen or more of the super-religious members hastened up front and fell upon their knees around Maye, loudly joining in her petition for mercy. Old Albert just slowly moved out a bit from the deacon's bench and stood intently watching the activity.

Back in the crowd, Clyde dropped his head, looking a bit sheepish—or maybe he was showing his disappointment. His wife, standing next to him, looked intently at him, thinking that maybe he was about to repent. But she had not long to look.

Up front, Maye had "prayed through" and was jumping up and down, shouting, "Glory, glory, glory!" In a moment she whirled and came up the aisle, shaking hands right and left, shouting all the while. When she reached the bench where Clyde sat, she paused, fastened her eyes on him, and called out, "Clyde, oh, Clyde! Run to that mourners' bench right now. You know you need to bad. Just as bad as I did, for you well know that me and you have committed adultery in about every laurel thicket on Long Creek, and all over my house too!" Then she shouted on up the aisle.

If Clyde had a desire to go to the mourners' bench, he had to delay a while. He was too busy fending off blows and slaps from his enraged wife, who was punctuating her physical attack upon her erring husband with shouted, unholy invectives.

But if poor Clyde thought he had lost his laurel-thicket partner to evangelical religion, he was wrong. When came warm spring, Maye took back to the thickets with him again, and was still doing so when I left Perry County and moved to Bristol, Tennessee, the following summer.

What the World Needs

Nearly all Pentecostal churches in the middle of the twentieth century held services on Saturday night. Some folks considered it the "devil's night," so I suppose the parishioners considered it a good time to give Old Scratch some competition. There were several guitars, a couple of fiddles, a banjo or two, and one mandolin, along with a piano, to provide foot-patting music. When all of these instruments mingled with a hundred or more people singing at the top of their voices, the rafters shook and the windows rattled. And usually before two songs had ended, 15 or 20 persons would be dancing and shouting in the spirit. With all that spirited music, plus scores of members energetically patting (stomping would be a better term) their feet and clapping hands, few could refrain from doing the holy jig. After about 30 minutes, the congregation would pray loudly in unison, followed by what was usually a long and lively sermon.

To fully understand the implications made in this story, you must know that throughout the South—and I am sure elsewhere—the word *peter* is commonly used for *penis*. Doubtless, though, a few folks may have been reared in such a strict religious environment that they do not know the slang term, which likely was the case with Florence Gibbons, an Assembly of God minister who pastored a country church in Calhoun County, Mississippi.

Sister Florence, as she was affectionately known by her many followers, had founded the greatly prospering church when she was an evangelist. The membership had reached perhaps a hundred or more at the time she had her "foot in mouth" episode.

On that particular Saturday night, a large crowd assembled, in spite of the steamy, torrid heat. Sister Florence, a rather large, Amazon type of woman, took the stand and launched into a powerful sermon on the courage of Peter. Her almost coarse voice had a tremendous volume, and she bore down heavily on Peter's hard-headed stand. Then she pictured him as a long, tall saint, fearless in purpose, and sticking with his duty until he finished his work. Casting her eyes toward Heaven and swinging her arms around, she boomed out:

"I tell you, saints, what this world needs is lots more good, long, strong, hard-headed Peters that'll get right in the middle of it, and stay with it till the job's done. Why, they's lots of Peters right here tonight that's a-wanting to get up and get with it. But, God help you, you just don't have the courage. Why, if you would just get up and do what you were made to do, it would do the world a lot of good. So get up, Peters, and do your job."

Her earnest urging was followed by a quick outburst of *amen*s, an outburst that died aborning. Many of the women suddenly realized what they seemed to be endorsing, so they cut off in mid-word or mid-phrase. The drop in volume was dramatic.

Then in the midst of it all, Sister Florence's husband, Joe Gibbons, who apparently had not been reared in a sheltered Christian environment, yelled, "Lord, have mercy, wife, what are you saying? You've shore done played the devil."

That apparently was the fuse that set the crowd off. The place roared with laughter. The shrieks of mirth from the more worldly women and the loud guffaws of unsanctified men fairly shook the crude church house to its foundation.

Sister Florence went silent and looked all around in puzzlement; she couldn't figure out what had happened. When she got a chance to speak, she avowed that the devil had come into the place, and she called for all to get down on their knees and help pray the devil out of the church.

But before the prayers started, someone from the worldly section of the church (the back two rows) shouted, "Why try to pray the devil out, Sister Florence, when you let him in?!"

There wasn't much spirit in the prayers that followed.

NOTE: One time near Harrison, Boone County, Arkansas, I heard a preacher almost fall into this same "trap." Fortunately, he caught himself in time and smoothed it over, but not before two or three of the brothers realized what was about to come and began to smile. So watch it, preachers, when you speak on Peter.

SETTING THE EXAMPLE

During depression times, cotton picking didn't pay much—about 50¢ per hundred pounds—but plenty of eager workers could be found. A very few might earn $1.50 per day, if willing to go early and work late. For the residents of Clarksville, Arkansas, the job required a four-mile journey to the Spadra bottoms, often on foot.

Among those who showed up regularly was Granny Stanton. Though nearly 80 years old, she could easily hold her own. She was a tall woman, but she could bend her back right along with the youngest workers. Frequently bringing home the coveted $1.50, she was proud of her ability to gather in the white gold.

During one hot and dry fall, her church, noted as the wildest holiness church in town, opened a protracted revival meeting. The services were long, lively, and exciting. But Granny Stanton attended every night, in spite of long hours spent in the Spadra bottoms and the four-mile walk in both directions. She would sing, shout, and do the holy dance until midnight or later, then be up before daybreak for the long hike to the cotton fields.

As the week wore on, many of the church members, who were also among her fellow cotton pickers, began to yield to the temptation to skip church and go to bed early. One night there were but few in attendance.

Testimony time came as usual, and Granny Stanton was the first to hit the floor. "Praise Jesus for this here revival," she began, " but I see lots of the saints have laid out tonight. I don't see why they can't be here. Oh, they claim they can't work hard all day and come out here and worship the dear Lord at night. Land, they ain't got much of a excuse. Look at me. I'm rat [right] old, and I done padded to Spadra and back and worked like a sonofabitch all day, and I'm here!"

BIG BELLE BAINES GETS THE BLESSING

Red Rock Point, rising to majestic heights over the Big Creek Valley, can be viewed from a great portion of eastern Newton County, Arkansas, and from far across the Big Buffalo River, which flows by a short distance to the north. Many men and women have been born, grown to old age, and died in nearby communities, including Piercetown, Mount Judea, Hasty, and Vendor. But while seeing this mountain almost daily, most of them have never been anywhere near to standing atop of it. Not so with Batson "Bat" Baines.

He grew up south of Jasper and as a youth, in his words, "picked huckleberries rat down, pert nigh to the jumpin-off place of that mountain." Soon after his first marriage, he moved to a home in clear sight of Red Rock Point. While not a resident of any of the aforementioned communities, and being several miles distant, he became a leader in a staid denominational church there.

His property contained the best spring of water in the neighborhood, and for that reason, when preacher Tom Biggs from Morrilton came looking for a place to build a brush arbor, the land near the spring was his first and natural choice. Bat Baines readily consented and spent days feeling good about his generosity. Evidently his own church did not feel so good about his act, however. At the next business meeting, he was excluded from the fellowship because of his aid to an "off brand" preacher.

Biggs was known as a "three-pump preacher," meaning that old-fashioned gas lamps had to be pumped three times before his message ended. He had "torn a strip" (made a big showing) in Pope, Conway, and Van Buren counties before landing near Pindall and, from there, into the hills in sight of Red Rock Point. His cardinal doctrine was that of a "powerful, soul-shaking, life-changing, mind-staggering second blessing." Indeed, he was trying to establish what he called The Church of the Second Blessing Saints of Jerusalem.

Now, the hills of north Arkansas are a long way from Jerusalem, making some wonder about the last part of that name, but I guess it sounded right holy, and that was reason enough for Biggs—though he didn't always have a reason for what he did. So he built a huge brush arbor near Bat Baines's spring and started the first of many revivals in that area.

Biggs had been a "kingpin banjo picker," and he didn't quit it after his conversion but had carried that talent into his ministry. To top it all, his slim, tall wife was a "string burner fiddler," who proudly stated, "Mah Uncle John learned me how."

She had joined her husband in providing music fit to raise the dead. That, coupled with fiery, bench-jumping, pole-climbing, dust-raising preaching, soon began to bring great numbers of those who liked their religion a little lively from near and far, even beyond Red Rock Point.

By the time of that first meeting, Bat had become a widower and had remarried a woman from near Fodder Stack Mountain. Belle, his second wife, stood around six feet tall and weighed almost three hundred pounds. She was highly emotional, impulsive, plain, and crude mouthed, but she was also a good worker and could cook country grub that would make you wish you could live and have good teeth for two hundred years.

At the start of the meeting, Belle sat beside Bat on a back bench near the big spring. As the services grew more energetic night after night, she began moving up closer, about a bench every night, leaving her more-amused-than-interested husband sitting alone in the back. Old sisters whispered to one another that Belle was getting conviction and was going to get so close that she would "fall in" before long.

On the first Saturday night after the meeting commenced, the crowd was especially large. "Tom Biggs was rarin' to go, and the meetin' started in high gear," was the way Bat Baines later described it. That banjo began whanging, and the fiddle added its shrill wail to the rousing songs. There was much hand clapping, and before the second song ended, men and women all over the arbor were in the aisles and between the benches, shouting and doing the holy dance. And with that foot-patting music and spirited singing, it must have been hard for stern old Bat to refrain from shaking a leg.

A drunk from somewhere back toward Western Grove wandered in, and seeing the high stepping of several of the crowd and hearing the spirited music, he mistakenly thought he had arrived at a Saturday night dance. Jumping up on the end of a bench, he called out, "Choose your partner, circle eight, swing that gal like swinging on a gate." Only a few near him heard his unseemly call.

In a moment he jumped down and grabbed Lucy Lee, who was doing a holy jig in the aisle. Thinking a dear brother was in the spirit, she swung around with him a few times. When she realized he was drunk, she tensed her corn-hoeing arms and shoved him with such vigor that he went tumbling into the dark at the edge of the arbor.

About that time, Big Belle Baines sprang up from the front bench and made a high dive onto the mourners' bench. That great victory sent the crowd into a thunderous uproar. Old Bat stiffened and about swallowed his tobacco.

A great portion of the crowd surged forward and dropped around the altar like hawks making for a fat hen convention. There they raised a mighty wail toward Heaven for the infilling (becoming full of the Holy Ghost) of sister Belle. Some beat the air, others beat the bench, and those close enough beat the back of the mourner, all the while screaming and calling out for the power to come down.

Preacher Biggs jumped up on the mourners' bench and quit his banjo picking long enough to yell out, "Folks, we've got down a rat smart of pare [power], but you'ns pray harder, and hit'll be a sight what'll happen." He then lit into his five stringer like the drivers on an express engine going ninety miles an hour. His wife came nearer and sawed into her fiddle with vigor to match her husband's. (I suppose they thought some music would help the coming of the second blessing.)

Meanwhile, Belle's three-hundred-pound frame was sprawled out over the crude pine bench, and she moaned and rolled her eyes like a calf soon to be in the great clover fields above. Suddenly she trembled, stiffened, and jumped wildly into the air. When she hit the ground, she let out a yell that could have been heard to the Buffalo valley. Then she lunged far left, then right, and back and forth.

"Lordy, oh, Lordy!" she shouted. "Hit's got me, eeowee, hit's got me."

"You mean, *you've* got *hit*!" Biggs bellowed out as he jumped stiff legged back and forth across the bench, never missing a note on his banjo. His wife went into a whirling dance but played her fiddle right on.

Mack Maness threw his cane into the air and began jumping in a circle as if he were nearer 16 than the 86 he actually was. He shouted as he went, spraying those nearby with well-processed tobacco juice. His wife, "Aunt" Cinda Maness, raised the arbor with a wild whoop or two and then jumped into an open space, doing the Virginia flatfoot, the pigeon wing, and the Charleston backstep, all in one.

Walsie Winkler threw her songbook straight up and began a stiff-legged jump over benches and down the aisle. Nona Neil rolled on the ground, kicking her heels high in the air, as Nora Walker threw her bonnet into her timid husband's lap and cried out, "Jist watch me do the glory hump!" And hump she did!

Meanwhile, Big Belle was charging around through the crowd like she had gone "slap dab" (completely and unquestionably) crazy. Time after time, she yelled, "Hit got me again," as she smacked at her side and front.

"Lordy," Walsie Winkler squalled out, "she's gonna get so holy, she'll fly off."

About that time, Belle saw an opening in the crowd and made for her husband like a hound dog after a greased biscuit. Those along her path fell back, for I guess they didn't want to be holy and hurt at the same time. She jumped and jumped, loudly screeching, "Get it, Bat, yeooow, get it!"

That riled him, for he thought she meant for him to get the second blessing, and he was well pleased with the first one. "Don't believe in sich blame foolishment," he growled out.

"You cussed old devil, I don't mean the blessin'," Belle snapped back as she smacked her side again. "There's a damned hornet up mah dress, and the sumbitch is a-stinging the hell out of me."

With another wild whoop, she lunged toward the darkness and the brush, throwing her clothes off as she went. And the crowd slowly realized that Big Belle wasn't sanctified after all.

Now, this writer has noticed that what appears as holy often is something else!

LESSER OF TWO EVILS

Between Jasper and Harrison, Arkansas, at the edge of Dogpatch, U.S.A. (a theme park that closed in the mid-1990s), is a large spring that sends its abundant flow of water into Mill Creek and eventually into the beautiful Big Buffalo River. In a little bottom near this spring once stood an open-air tabernacle, where my great-uncle Ab Phillips held his annual Methodist Camp Meetings over a century ago.

He owned the large mill just below Marble Falls and also had a prosperous mercantile nearby. But every summer he curtailed his business activities and preached for weeks in the tabernacle. Hundreds came from the surrounding hills, hollows, and distant valleys to attend.

The crowds that gathered in that valley later to see the attractions of Dogpatch did not realize that a hundred years earlier similar crowds assembled there, attracted by a capable, qualified preacher and a large, open-air shed.

Toward the turn of the century, Ab suffered a series of financial reverses, forcing him to leave Marble Falls. For years after his move across the hills to Jasper on the Little Buffalo River, he would occasionally return to Marble Falls and hold a protracted revival meeting. The tabernacle was gone, so the meetings were held in the local schoolhouse (the building still stood when I was there in 1981, occupied by a Masonic lodge).

One of the meetings was especially successful. Folks traveled for miles, night after night, many of them former attendants of the tabernacle meetings. As wagons and buggies parked in the schoolyard, occupants would alight from them shouting and embracing one another. Sometimes hymns began in the yard and caused a breakout of revival fires long before the hour of service. Inside the sweltering schoolhouse, the first hymn often brought so many mourners to the front that no preaching could be had.

One night the weather was unusually hot and oppressive—so hot that one old-timer said the lightning bugs had extinguished their lights with their own sweat. Now, that's pretty hot for north Arkansas or anywhere else, but it did not stop the rousing singing of hymns and a long and persuasive sermon from Ab. Finally the preaching ended, and he led the congregation in singing "Come Ye Sinners, Poor and Needy."

From the back of the crowded room, a lanky teenage boy came quickly forward. He was well-known in the area, and the schoolhouse was filled with his relatives and friends. His coming forward set women to shouting and strong men to weeping. When he threw himself upon the mourners' bench, a crowd flocked around him like chickens after a throw of corn. A volley of prayers bombarded Heaven in behalf of the young man, as many beat the altar or lifted waving hands above their heads.

One lady around the overcrowded mourners' bench was Tressie Treat from nearby P D Flat, who invariably brought a large palm-leaf fan with her. That night she stood directly behind the mourner, swinging her fan over him and pleading to Heaven for his salvation. (I've always thought that one ought to swing a fan as well as pray if the need be, for I haven't yet seen the Lord do the fanning when others are around to do it!)

After a while, old sister Treat became worried. The crowd was closing in, the air was heavy, and the sweat was pouring. She straightened up and began sweeping her extended arms backward, elbowing and pushing the crowd back. "Stand back, folks!" she cried out. "Stand back and give 'im air. He might as well die and go to hell as to smother to death!"

Well, he didn't smother to death or go anywhere, either, for he was a fine Christian gentleman and my neighbor when I lived in Harrison, Arkansas, in the early 1970s.

MAD DOG SUMMER

The summer of 1937 was extremely hot, and a weeks-long drought had parched the Limestone Valley in lower Newton County, Arkansas. As often happens at such times, that deep mountain valley had a mad-dog scare. Two or three had been sighted locally, causing the residents to take drastic precautions to avoid the frightful animals.

Being bitten and infected with the dreadful rabies would certainly prove fatal. Virtually everyone had heard horror stories of the awful results of the supposedly incurable scourge. Most of the local folks, careful to arrive home before dark, closed their doors and windows tight in spite of the oppressive heat. Livestock was herded into barns to prevent them from being bitten by rabid animals. Parents warned their children to watch carefully on their way to or from school for dogs behaving strangely. It was a scary time for Limestone Valley, and many nearby communities were also in a state of terror because of the widespread rabies.

In the midst of all this, Sam Allen announced that he would preach in the Upper Limestone schoolhouse come Sunday morning and Sunday night. A leader in the community sent him word to expect a few on Sunday morning, but he doubted if there would be "enough to hold J. P. court" on Sunday night. Sam felt that the Gospel ought to be preached anyway, mad dogs or no mad dogs, so on Saturday he rode his horse down from his home high on Parker's Ridge to spend the night in a valley home, so as to be ready for the next day's meetings.

Now, Sam Allen, who had been preaching in that section for well over fifty years, was greatly loved and respected by virtually all who knew him. He could draw a large crowd, though others could not muster up a couple dozen people, if that many.

Even at his advanced age of about 85, he could still preach an exciting message. It might take him a good thirty minutes to "get steamed up," but once he did, he would charge back and forth across the stage, down and around the pulpit, and sometimes up and down the aisles, bellowing and shouting out thrilling portions of the scriptures.

If perchance he stood in one spot for a minute or two, he would place his hands on his back and put one foot forward and pat it to the tune of his preaching. Tune, indeed; one person who frequently heard him said that though the old brother often got to preaching so fast that the words couldn't be understood, the tune sounded good anyway.

Actually it was the Arkansas style of that "holy tone" so loved by the Kentucky Baptists and practiced by Irby Hale as described earlier in this book. I last heard Sam Allen in May 1945, but in my memory, I can still hear that old mountain preacher singsonging out the Gospel.

On that particular Sunday morning, in spite of the mad-dog scare, a large crowd gathered at the Upper Limestone schoolhouse. There were a few automobiles in the area at the time, but most folks still traveled by wagon, buggy, or horseback. Many simply walked to the meeting place. They came from all over the valley, some from as far down as Fort Douglas and Beech Grove (the latter is the native community of this writer) and as far up as Walnut Fork, Deer Mountain, and Hurricane Creek.

Some of the men carried guns, not just to hunt along the way, but also as mad dog protection. A few folks carried clubs, including "Aunt" Nora Burris, who hoofed it all the way from Parker's Ridge. She didn't have an actual club, mind you, but that dear old woman carried a fence rail over her shoulder. "I'll make souse meat outen any mad dog I meet," she had boasted to someone along the way.

The singing that morning sounded angelic. Most of those people were "all keyed up to shake the rafters," since they had not been at a good meeting for a month or more. "Aunt" Rosey Davis, who lived just across the road from the schoolhouse, had allowed her pump organ to be brought over to provide a little accompaniment with the singing. Though she had never had a lesson in her life, she could make that old organ "talk." So she provided the music that morning for some lively hill-country singing.

She was what some called a "walking cotton bale" in those parts; that is, she was extremely fat. When she sat on that small organ stool, more of her was hanging over the edges than was being supported. The sight was a matter of amusement to the younger set and likely to several of the older folks, as well.

All that music and singing got old Sam Allen steamed up. When his time came, he hit the floor in high gear. In no time, he was charging all over the stage and up and down the aisles, waving his arms and bellowing out the Gospel message. It looked like folks were going to have an exciting meeting. Indeed, they did—but not exactly in the way expected.

As things became spirited inside the schoolhouse, a little mischief was brewing in the schoolyard with a dozen or more teenage boys. Regarded as the roughnecks or rowdies of the community, they were capable of just about anything.

A leader among them, tall, lanky Johnny Cleburne from Rosetta Mountain, had come to the meeting that morning trailed by his big yellow dog, Old George. As the boys milled about in the shade near the schoolhouse, the dog rested quietly at the side of the play yard, near the big spring that supplied water for the school and several nearby homes.

Johnny eyed Old George, hoping rabies would never strike his canine companion, and suddenly got an idea for a little fun. He turned to one of the boys, who lived within sight of the school, and asked, "Has your pa got a shaving cup, soap, and brush?"

"Why, shore," the boy replied. "All shavin' folks does."

Then Johnny whispered his plan, and the boy ran to his nearby home. Once Johnny had the necessary equipment in hand, he dipped the brush in the spring and soon worked up a good lather. He took the dog to the blind side of the schoolhouse (the side with no windows) and soaped Old George's muzzle with a lavish amount of foaming suds.

Winking at the amused boys standing by, he then led Old George to the school's only door, whispered "sic 'em," and gave the somewhat bewildered dog a shove right down the center aisle. The brazen boy then shouted out in what sounded like a genuinely terrorized voice, "Lawsy, look out, they is a mad dog a-comin'!"

At that point, Sam Allen, hands on back, was standing by the lectern,

sing-songing out promises concerning the coming kingdom, and doing his usual foot pat. The crowd was with him, and some were just about to shout, when that dread call "mad dog comin'" was yelled out even louder than Sam was preaching. And the warning was quickly followed by the loud yelping and barking of Old George as he charged down the aisle toward the greatly startled preacher.

The effect was horrendous. Sam stopped in mid-sentence, cried out, "Great Gawd have mercy," and whirled and began frantically searching for a back door that didn't exist. He then jumped backwards upon a bench against the wall back of the pulpit, trying desperately to stop the oncoming dog by rebuking him in the name of the Lord.

But there wasn't much time for rebuking to work. By then, Old George had sprung upon the stage and seemed to be trying to decide whether to go for the preacher or Aunt Rosey Davis, who had bounded up from her overburdened stool and was jumping up and down screaming. When it looked like the dog preferred her, she grabbed the stool and made a wild swing at him.

Old George lunged at her, and she fell backward into the organ, which was on the edge of the stage. Being rammed by so much weight, it toppled over and hit the main floor with a tremendous crash. The noise greatly startled and frightened the already bewildered dog, so he began leaping high in the air and snapping his teeth. That gave the audience a good view, allowing them to see the foam apparently flowing from his mouth. If there had been any doubt that the dog was rabid, it was now removed.

The crowd, which had sat in stunned silence to that point, suddenly came to life. There were terrified shouts of "run for your lives" as all bedlam broke loose. Run they did, soon clogging the only doorway. Those who could get to the windows began climbing out. One big, old, 300-pound woman jumped up on an already sagging bench, which immediately snapped and sent her tumbling to the floor. People began hurdling over her to get to the window at the end of her bench.

It is truly amazing what people will do when in a completely terrorized frame of mind. Not all choose to run. "Long" Bill Bacum, from way up in Walnut Valley, remained seated, calmly drew a pistol from his pocket, and began shooting—not at the supposed mad dog, but at the ceiling. After emptying the gun, he dropped it and remained seated, staring straight ahead.

Aunt Nora Burris hopped up but did not flee. She began swinging the rail she had carried all the way from Parker's Ridge, mowing down anyone unfortunate enough to be within its reach. That swinging rail actually did more damage than the supposed mad dog.

Meanwhile, Old George, frightened as much as were the people, made for Sam Allen. The preacher, with one wild vault, sailed right over the dog and tore down the aisle, with the animal in hot pursuit. If the doorway was clogged, Preacher Allen unclogged it! The schoolhouse was empty in nothing flat.

The poor dog just raced around outside not knowing what to do. And some who fled noticed that those yard boys didn't seem to be afraid of the "mad dog" at all. Indeed, some of the roughnecks were down in the yard rolling and shaking with fits of laughter.

A few days later, as two local women discussed the Sunday morning event, one of them said she was sure sorry that brother Allen didn't get to finish what she thought was going to be one of the best sermons she'd ever heard him preach.

The other woman immediately replied, "Well, now, I've done plumb lost faith in him."

Shocked, the first woman inquired why.

Fast came the reply: "Well, when we was all tryin' to git outen that schoolhouse at the same time, Preacher Allen knocked me sideways and pert nigh down in the floor. I could understand that, in that the dog was grabbing for his leg. But then I heard him rip out, 'To hell with any damned bunch of sonofbitches that'd build a schoolhouse with jist one door!'"

May I add that within a short time, a new door was installed at the back of that schoolhouse, near the speaker's stand.

PRANKSTER WIFE

I often wondered why there was always a vacant choir seat in front of the minister's wife, until a local parishioner finally told me.

The little Methodist church near Plum Branch, South Carolina, had an excellent choir, directed by their minister, who had been in his new charge only a brief time. Rev. Brownlow, then around 30 years of age, had recently married. The humble, dedicated, and effective minister had served several charges as a bachelor, but in each work, he increasingly felt the need for a wife. Perhaps he had become too anxious, for during his previous pastorate, he married a flippant young girl who was perhaps a dozen years his junior. True, she had been a loyal member of that former church, had helped in the work of the youth, and always gave her sweet voice to the choir. But she was a pronounced fun lover and a bit of a prankster.

In the new church, she had readily joined the choir. Directly in front of her sat old Jack Wells. He had attended faithfully for years and sang in the choir, but he had never joined the church, nor did he make any profession of being religious. Yet, he was highly respected and loved by everyone in the surrounding community.

For some reason, the minister's wife thought of how funny it would be to jam a needle through the opening in the choir seat into the most likely part of Jack's anatomy. She had many laughs over what she imagined might be the result of such an act. She thought on it more and more until it became an irresistible urge with her.

On a balmy mid-May morning, the congregation eagerly gathered at the little chapel in the red-clay-hill piney woods near Plum Branch. And no one would even suspect that the young Mrs. Brownlow carried her secret weapon in her purse. Seated in the choir, she had a hard time holding a pious look during the opening hymns.

Time came for meditation and prayer, and the organist lowered the volume to "funeral tones" as the worshipers bowed their heads and closed their eyes. The moment had arrived. Mrs. Brownlow looked left and right, saw no one watching, and swiftly drew forth the long needle from her purse. Jack's pants were pulled tight, making a clear target. Easing the needle into position, the minister's wife was seized with a moment of anxious hesitation, but courage returned to her and, with a sudden jab, she drove the needle deep.

Jack sprang quickly from his seat, yelled at the top of his voice, and broke wind loudly as he jumped forward, slapping at the seat of his pants. Then in embarrassment and pain, he lunged for the side door, crying out, "Oh, hells be damned!"

And the stunned congregation could not help but notice that the young Mrs. Brownlow was doubled up in spasms of shaking, silent laughter. Jack Wells never returned to the church, and no one would ever sit in front of the minister's wife again for as long as her husband served the congregation.

ONLY TWO WISE MEN

Oak Flats School, which also served as the community church, held a big Christmas pageant every year. Everyone in that remote section of Caldwell County, North Carolina, looked forward to the program, which regularly featured the appearance of the wise men at the Bethlehem stable. The maiden schoolteacher, who for most of her adult years had held sway over the one-room school, particularly delighted in directing that portion of the play. In it, as well as all other matters, she about demanded perfection.

Miss Anna abhorred the idea of her wise men putting on robes over bulky and protruding clothing. One time she had, with horror, seen a rolled-up pant leg slowly descend from under the robe of one of her actors. Deeply vexed, she issued the order that the boys strip to the skin before wearing their robes. But to maintain modesty, she required that the boys wear tight swim trunks, just in case a robe might fall open at the wrong moment.

Local youth felt honored if chosen to represent one of those ancient travelers. One year, Miss Anna picked Luther "Luke" Hoskins, an eighth grader from way back on Buck Mountain, to portray the lead wise man. The other two were a couple of lads from a grade or two down. For weeks she drilled them endlessly, hoping to put on a never-to-be-forgotten performance. Her hopes were realized but not in the way she expected.

Luke had turned 16 five months earlier, but at that young age, he stood a full six feet tall and was as developed as a 21-year-old. Indeed, his maturity was so apparent that mothers in the community had protectively passed the word around not to let their daughters get loose with Luke, "fer he's done got dangerous early." And Luke, aware of his advanced and very pronounced manhood, had become something of an exhibitionist.

On the big night, the actors gathered early, so that they might conceal themselves from the gathering crowd. Nails had been driven into both sides of the schoolroom, and a heavy curtain hung from wires strung between the nails. On either side of the stage, more wires led to the back wall, and from these, Miss Anna hung short curtains to partition off dressing rooms. Luke and the other boys dressed on the left side.

While the crowd assembled in the little community building, this young lad was not hastening to put on his robe. Rather, he strutted around in the nude, before the two younger boys who were to serve with him. But the fact that he was not ready to play to a full house and mixed audience soon became apparent.

A hush fell over the room as Miss Anna arose and gave opening remarks to the expectant congregation. Finally she reached back and, with a graceful sweep, opened the curtains, indicating that the program was about to begin. But Luke, knowing that his part was not yet to be presented, still strutted around behind the dressing room curtain.

Alas, someone had not driven the nail deep enough. Over by the left wall, there was first a tremor, and then the main wire gave way, suddenly bringing down not only the front curtain, but those of the dressing areas as well. Yes, there were two wise men fully robed and standing near their entry point. And there was Luke, standing in full view of the startled crowd, as naked as the day he was born. He appeared a bit stunned.

For a long moment, he stood still as a statue, then gave a yell as the truth hit him. He lunged left and right, grabbing for robe, curtain, whatever. He finally seized his robe, but somehow it became tangled around his feet, and down he went. He was up instantly and whirled toward the wall. Then, realizing that the crowd had a good back view, he spun again, only to expose his entire front.

There was only one thing to do—flee—but the room had no back door. So he ran down the main aisle, yelling, "Turn out the lights! Oh, dammit, somebody turn out the damn lights!"

But no one obeyed, and his frantic flight to and through the front door was in the bright glare of the overhead bulbs. A few women and girls covered their faces, but not many. Men cackled, and girls tee-heed, as Luke dashed by. And not a few mothers silently noted that their warning that Luke had "done got dangerous early" was by no means a false alarm.

Miss Anna somehow managed to whip the program back together and continue on. But only two wise men appeared at the Bethlehem stable.

RIGHTEOUS INDIGNATION

J. M. Shinn started out as a small-town lawyer near Harrison in Boone County, Arkansas. He worked his way up and finally became the circuit judge of his district. After retiring from the judgeship, he continued to practice law in Harrison and the surrounding proximity. Because of his legal expertise, he was engaged in the "big" cases of his day. Naturally he made many enemies—both as a judge and as a lawyer—but even his worst enemies had a certain respect for him.

My family considered him a cousin of sorts. Judge Shinn had been converted as a young man under the preaching of my great-uncle Absolom C. Phillips, who later became his father-in-law. Rev. Phillips was an old-time, sanctified, no-nonsense, shouting Methodist minister, and much of his belief and lifestyle was adopted by young Mr. Shinn.

As the lawyer advanced in his career and later became a judge, religious principles played a major role in his court decisions, and he often diligently searched the Bible for help in making important legal determinations. Admonishing many on trial before him to repent and seek a better life, he earned the moniker "the preaching judge."

Judge Shinn was long a faithful member of the First Methodist Church in Harrison. Eventually he was given the teachership of the rather large adult Bible class, and he well filled the position for many years. Indeed, attendance greatly increased under the learned, capable, and interesting teacher.

Though he always seemed devout, rumors circulated that, under enough pressure, Judge Shinn would cuss a little. Some believed the rumor, while others strongly doubted it. The matter was finally settled in an unexpected manner.

Near Easter one year, the class lesson centered on the trial and crucifixion of Jesus Christ, a lesson made for the jurist. Often he mixed his education in legalism with the teachings of Jesus Christ, and on that day he went all out. The more he spoke on the error-ridden, illegal, rigged, and unjust trial of Jesus, the hotter waxed his righteous indignation. His face reddened and his voice boomed louder and louder. Holding the Bible in one hand and swinging his free arm, he proceeded to lambaste those who had pulled the treacherous strings in what he called a mock trial.

Finally he bellowed out, "Why, those who tried Christ ought themselves to have been on trial. Yes, indeed! And I would like mighty well to have been the judge who tried the damned, low down, sons of bitches."

You may be sure that no one in attendance ever forgot that Sunday school lesson!

HE KEPT ON DANCING AFTER THE MUSIC STOPPED

Soon after the members of Central Presbyterian Church erected their first building in downtown Bristol, Virginia, the congregation purchased an organ. The fine church-type organ had to be hand pumped—no electricity was available at the time—but instead of foot pedals, as was standard on parlor organs, it was pumped from behind with a two-handled pump similar to those once used to inflate car tires.

When air was needed, the organist pulled out a handle above the keyboard. This raised a red flap on the back of the organ, under which was a white disk with the word *air* stamped in bold letters at its center. The raising of the flap was accompanied by a faint ding, the signal for the pumper to start what hopefully would be a steady and strong current of air through the music chamber of the organ.

The cramped, hot-in-summer, cold-in-winter position behind the organ did not constitute ideal working conditions, to say the least. The hard, steady pumping that had to be done through long Presbyterian hymns was by no means an easy task and required a lot of stamina and persistence.

At first, volunteers from the congregation took the duty of pumping, but this soon proved undependable. Seldom did a volunteer last through a month of services. Finally, the board of elders decided to hire outside help, so, a bit reluctantly, they allotted four dollars per month for this purpose.

The first person employed as a pumper was Judson Meek, a precocious, muscular boy about 16 or 17 years old. His rather poor family lived in the notorious Burson Row, a slum section adjoining what is now the south side of Rice Terrace. The four dollars per month likely meant much to a lad who had never had a dollar of his own in his entire life. The job also brought him under the influence of a church and may have helped stabilize his somewhat topsy-turvy existence.

Following instructions, he always arrived early and took his place behind the organ. When the service ended, he quietly slipped out the side door and hurried home. Sunday after Sunday, when that red tag flipped up and the little ding sounded, he seized the pump and manfully did his duty, never seen by the congregation. The organist at the time, Jeanne English Baumgardner, once commented that Judson did a better job of keeping a steady and strong flow of air through the organ than had any of the volunteers who'd served before him.

Everything went smoothly for several months, until a never-to-be-forgotten morning in June when the congregation got their first view of the organ pumper. And that first view was vividly remembered by some church members when this writer came to Bristol in 1953.

On that bright Sunday, he took his usual place and waited patiently for the "give it air" signal. The first hymn was a Presbyterian favorite, "How Firm a Foundation." At about the beginning of the third verse, the "show" began.

Young Judson was wearing bell-bottom trousers that day. When he knelt on the cushion to begin pumping, his trouser legs flared out upon the floor, forming perfect tunnels for anything that might creep by. It so happened that a mouse came silently scurrying across the floor that morning and raced right up one of those tunnels!

The lad suddenly stiffened and jumped high, thus opening the tunnel past his knee and allowing the mouse to quickly continue his journey upward. By the time the mouse reached mid-thigh, the music had stopped, but the boy kept on dancing! And what a frantic, hopping, leg-shaking dance it was. Though not accompanied by music, it was accompanied by shouts, shrieks, and even a few curses. (Perhaps the church influence had not been so great after all.)

He danced from behind the organ, still yelling and kicking, madly shaking his leg and clawing at his pants. As his fright reached the panic stage, he did more than claw at his pants—he jerked and kicked them off! Thus the first view of the organ pumper by that greatly startled congregation was unobstructed, to say the least. Unobstructed indeed, for like most youth of the time, especially the poorer set, he wore no underwear.

But that wasn't all the show. The mouse, freed at last, leaped to the floor and sailed under the feet of Fannie Lin English, a sister of the organist. When it brushed her ankle, she thought it was running up her leg. She sprang up, screaming to high heaven, and joined in the dance. Luckily the mouse did not continue its ascension act, or there might have been another striptease show.

By that time, the organ pumper, released from the source of his terror, suddenly realized his bare condition. He began lunging about, desperately looking for the nearest exit. The side door was standing open, and he dashed through it into the street, where he realized he was exposed to the public without his pants. He ran back into the church and grabbed his pants; holding them before him, he raced again out the door and up Moore Street toward home.

Well, the law must be followed. In a dusty old book now stored in the basement of the Washington County Courthouse in Abingdon, Virginia, can be found a notation that tells the rest of the story. Judson Meek duly appeared before the chief justice of the county court and was fined five dollars (suspended) for indecent exposure, disturbing public worship, and uttering profane and blasphemous oaths—and that on the sabbath day.

The late Dad Thomas once told me that the boy, shamed by all this, left his home and wandered for a time over the deep South, finally settling in Mississippi. One wonders if he ever again danced without music.

Scripture Didn't Sound Right

Joe King, a traveling evangelist, roamed all over northwestern South Carolina, preaching wherever and whenever the opportunity arose. And he offered more than hellfire-and-brimstone preaching. He expertly played the accordion and invariably included a medley of tunes before his sermons. The simple songs—he wrote many of them himself—always contained a message that was usually well received by those who came to his rather lively revivals.

He carried his highly prized accordion in a leather-bound, red-velvet-lined case, which he usually placed on the floor near the pulpit, ready to receive his treasured instrument when the musical part of his service ended. He handled his accordion like a baby, usually taking time to carefully place it in and close the case before beginning his sermon.

One summer, King wandered into Anderson, South Carolina, the largest city in which he had ever preached. I suppose he was a bit proud of this "promotion," for he certainly pulled out all the stops when singing and preaching there. The meetings, held in a little neighborhood Holiness church, drew large crowds from the first. They grew nightly, which greatly pleased him and doubtless helped "steam him up."

He was so steamed up one night that he began preaching with the accordion still strapped around his neck. Finding that somewhat confining—he liked to dart about and fight the air as he preached—he slipped it off, preaching all the while, and did not take time to put it in the open case. Instead he placed it on his chair directly behind the pulpit.

The crowd that night, so large that many had to sit up on the stage in a semicircle around the preacher, included a young man who was in charge of two little "wild" boys. He may have been in charge, but he wasn't having much luck keeping them in place. The more engrossed he became with the sermon about the raising of Lazarus from the dead, the more the little fellows ran about the stage. Finally one of the youngsters spied the open accordion case and jumped right in. He began a twisting dance, but most of the people, including those sitting on the stage, were too enthralled with the lively sermon to notice.

Then the preacher reached the place where Jesus stood before the open tomb ready to call forth the dead Lazarus. He quoted the 42nd verse of the 11th chapter of the Book of St. John. Then, launching right into the 43rd, he bellowed, "And when he thus had spoken, he cried with a loud voice—" At that instant he swung around and with horror saw the lad dancing around in his cherished accordion case. And with barely a pause, as if he were finishing the verse he had begun, King boomed out, "Why, you little devil, get out of there!"

One old brother, who sat half asleep on a front pew yet heard every word, jerked awake and in a clearly audible voice said, "Why, that don't sound just right."

The sermon continued on to a hasty finish, but somehow Joe King had lost his steam.

Dogs Take Communion

Nearly two centuries have passed since the establishment of Oven Fork Regular Baptist Church on the Cumberland River in Letcher County, Kentucky. My great-great-grandfather Samuel Maggard was a charter member, and my great-grandfather James Maggard once served as moderator (pastor). And it has long been "loaded" with other members of my mother's family and still is to this day.

Doubtless many interesting events have taken place in that church during her long history, and likely several of these events have been a bit humorous. But perhaps most memorable is when some dogs once took Communion.

Far back, folks used real wine and unleavened bread in the much-anticipated sacrament. It always fell the lot of some deacon's wife to bake a loaf of unleavened bread, and real wine was not hard to find on Cumberland. Wafers and grape juice, commonly used now in churches everywhere, would not have then been acceptable in that staid church.

On this particular occasion, Clarinda Kelley Lewis (wife of John J. Lewis) baked the bread. As usual, the big loaf, unwrapped and uncovered, sat upon a crude table near the pulpit, where the participants would break off tiny pieces at the end of the service.

Oven Fork held services only once a month, a practice that still continues. Not only did the moderator preach, but usually there were several visiting ministers, who, if they were of the same faith and order, would also be given the opportunity to speak their piece. Few ever failed to take advantage of this opportunity, and often their "piece" was long. (At my first visit to Oven Fork, seven ministers "took the stand" before the lengthy service ended.) Everyone expected that each service would last several hours, and that expectation was usually realized. Certainly it was on the day when the dogs took Communion.

As that long service dragged on, 6-year-old Marion Brown (a distant cousin of mine) became hungry. Though his grandmother had fed him a breakfast of biscuits and side meat before daylight, a growing boy can just about become desperate for food in that long a time. And desperate he must have been.

Sitting there on the front bench by his grandmother, he eyed the loaf of brown, crusty bread. Oh, it looked so good, and it began to look better as minister after minister spoke. As Marion stared at the loaf, a plan slowly formed in his young mind. He knew that often there were long prayers between speakers, during which time the devout usually sat with closed eyes. Why not slip up there and grab that bread, he wondered, then sail out the side door for a feast in the churchyard.

Well, prayer time came, and as everyone closed their eyes and bowed their heads, Marion eased from the bench and slipped up to the table. He had the loaf of bread in hand and was making a dash for the side door when his grandmother, alerted by his absence, jumped up. She lunged at him, yelling out, "Drop that bread, you little devil, drop that bread!"

The sudden and unexpected interruption in the solemn prayer time must have greatly startled the congregation. But Marion was not concerned about such things. Realizing that his grandmother almost had him, he thought he might yet have a chance to save the much-coveted bread. So he threw it out the side door and far into the yard, just as his grandmother grabbed him.

Out in the yard, three or four big dogs lay in the shade, patiently waiting for their masters to emerge from the meetinghouse. But the bread suddenly emerging likely looked far better to them. They all jumped up and made a grab for it. They soon tore it to bits, and they devoured those bits within seconds. And within seconds inside, Marion's grandmother had hold of him and was trying to administer the tanning of his life. Three or four times, the wiry child managed to break loose of her grip and make a wild dash for freedom. She would dash after him and catch him, and the scene would replay.

Once, she tripped over something and sprawled out in the floor, but she sprang up and caught him just before he cleared the side door. Another time she charged into the big potbellied stove and shook it so hard that the pipes fell, filling the air with black soot. It was quite a floor show for such a no-nonsense church. But in the end, the grandmother was victorious. Marion never forgot the walloping she gave him.

Now, getting back to the dogs: they had broken and eaten that holy bread and had thus taken Communion. At least the more worldly of the folks in attendance at Oven Fork made that facetious conclusion, and they have repeated it that way it for years.

WHAT HAVE I SAID?

The church near Collettsville, Caldwell County, North Carolina, was prospering greatly, and the 27-year-old pastor wanted to keep the trend going. So he invited the preacher of a neighboring church to come for a revival, hoping to increase the momentum even more. The revival started on Sunday night, August 25, 1957. (I recall the date because I attended that service and it was my birthday.)

The house was filled with an eager congregation, ready for a week of having their religion stirred up, and hoping for the conversion of their sinner friends and neighbors. Many nonmembers were present, including several from the visiting minister's church. The singing started with notable fervor that increased with every new selection—so much so that within a few minutes, several women had reached the shouting point, while men gave forth their hearty *amen*s.

The air seemed charged with optimistic expectation, which pleased the devout young pastor to the point of near ecstasy. When he arose to make the opening remarks and perhaps give an announcement or two, his face beamed with joy and victory.

"I just know this is going to be one of the greatest revivals ever held in Caldwell County," he began. "Thank God for great revivals! I remember that one right here in this church a few years ago, when I, a poor and very lost sinner came to the light. Land, I recall how the singing started off about like it did here tonight. And I recall with everlasting gratitude that dear old servant of God who had come here from over in Tennessee to preach salvation to us. May his sainted soul rest in peace tonight. He preached my soul under deep conviction.

"Then they started to sing some old invitation hymn," he continued. "I think it was 'Come Ye Sinners, Poor and Needy.' Oh, brothers and sisters tonight, I knew I had to run one way or the other. It was either run up here to this altar bench or out that door back there. The convicting power was on me strong; you who've been there know what I mean. Oh, my soul, my soul."

He was getting steamed up, and the crowd was with him. One old sister already had both hands high in the air, and folks knew she'd be shouting soon. Another woman screeched out, "Bless him, sweet Jesus." A brother or two yelled, "Amen! Praise the Lord!"

All of that just fired him up to a higher degree of his already high religious fervor. "I'm not gonna preach tonight," he went on, "but I'm going to take a little time to testify. Well, the devil had ahold of me real strong. Oh, I was so wicked, a rebel to the ways of God. So very full of the ways of hell, oh so many ways of hell. So I started to run for the door.

"But that good Holy Ghost that had flooded my soul with so strong conviction wasn't going to let me go. No he wasn't going to let me go. When I reached the door, that good Holy Ghost grabbed me. Yes, I mean grabbed me. I was stopped dead in my tracks.

"Lordy, I fell to my knees and went to shaking. Land, that Holy Ghost just shook all those hellish ways out of me, and sweet victory rolled down from Heaven, and I jumped up, and some of you remember how I just jumped and shouted all over this place."

That really set the crowd off. Three or four women leaped to their feet, jumping up and down and shouting to high heaven. A man or two joined them, and others called out, "Amen! Praise the Lord!" One or two managed to yell, "Yes, I was right here when that happened. Glory, glory!"

Inspired by the congregation, the young minister hopped up on the front pew. With evangelistic zeal clearly showing in his face, he bellowed out an exhortation so loud and strong that it was clearly heard over the praise still erupting all over the church.

"Now, I'm going to pray that you sinners will heed the Savior's call and come up here and be saved from your wicked ways. Don't resist the spirit to your own destruction. And I'm going to pray that if any of you plan to try to run out that door like I did, that the good Holy Ghost that grabbed me and just shook these hellish ways out of me will grab you and just shake the hell out of you."

Instantly he went quiet. His face darkened and he swallowed hard. A look of horror swept over his face as he realized the implication of what he had said. There was also a stunned silence in the crowd for a few moments. Those sitting on the front bench heard him lowly mutter, "Good Lord, what have I said."

An old lady from the visiting pastor's congregation became the fuse that set off the dynamite. The epitome of quiet dignity, sitting so upright and stiff as if she were in a straight jacket, she, too, looked stunned for a moment. Then she bent forward in a vain effort to hump down behind the pew before her suppressed mirth became too obvious. But she didn't make it. The inner pressure was too great, and she suddenly erupted in shrieking cackles that sounded like a barnyard hen laying an egg.

That did it! All over the church, others quickly followed suit, until the rafters fairly trembled with roars of exploding laughter. Others silently quivered with spasms of mirth. Some never completely regained their composure through what turned out to be a rather brief service.

Apparently, though, the devout, if overly zealous minister did not lose his standing with that church. Nearly half a century has slipped by, and at last report he was still the pastor and going strong.

THE GHOST WASN'T HOLY

The folks in the Wilson Creek section of Caldwell County, North Carolina, had experienced a great revival. Preacher Austin Brashears from adjoining Burke County had turned the local, somewhat standard, quiet church into what one former member described as a "wild, shouting, tongue-speaking bunch of zealots."

Indeed, the revival had been effective, with more than 60 converts—many of them reconverted from a far different faith that had long prevailed in the community. And even though the revival took place in midwinter, all converts and reconverts were baptized in the icy waters of Wilson Creek, which swiftly flowed down from the towering Grandfather Mountain. For most of them, it was a rebaptism, since Brashears insisted that all who got the "new light" must start over again—and starting over meant that they must go under the water a second time.

Water baptism wasn't all he stressed. He bore down heavily on a spiritual baptism, which he called "gettin' the Holy Ghost baptism of fire," evidenced by what locals called "speaking in the unknown tongue." And Brashears insisted that all new converts or reconverts seek to receive this baptism. He even went so far as to call those who remained without it "half-baked" Christians, putting a lot of pressure on his followers to conform to his teachings in the matter. Few resisted going another step on the "holy pathway to higher spiritual ground"; most everyone blindly followed their new ecclesiastical leader.

Long after the big revival ended and Brashears went on to other localities, folks in the various sections of the neighborhood often gathered for what they called cottage prayer meetings, with the purpose of "seeking the baptism of the Holy Ghost." The meetings usually went on for hours, with much spirited singing, praying, shouting, and individual testimonies.

Occasionally someone danced in the spirit or fell under the power and rolled in the floor. If a seeker "got through" and began to speak in tongues, a great demonstration of spiritual joy and power would erupt. Lots of folks came "just to see the show," as they called it. Not many left disappointed!

Most meetings took place at night, but a few were conducted in daytime, usually in the afternoon. One particular afternoon meeting—lively and exciting, but not in the usual manner—will never be forgotten.

"Uncle" Evan Clark and his wife, "Aunt" Maggie, lived in the largest and what once had been the most impressive residence on Wilson Creek, built by a northern timber dealer who had come into the community many years before. After he died, his family moved to various distant locations, leaving the structure vacant and standing wide open for several years. During that time it had been vandalized a great deal, but a bachelor brother of Evan Clark's finally bought it and again made it livable.

Rumors had circulated that the big old house was badly haunted. For one thing, the builder's son Willett had died of appendicitis at the age of 18 and had been buried on the hill above the dwelling. Some said that from time to time he came back from the dead to wander about the grounds and through the halls and rooms of the deserted home. Uncle Evan's brother had supposedly met the ghost several times. When the brother died, Evan inherited the house.

Now, Aunt Maggie was scared stiff of what she called hants. She would not stay in the residence alone, even in broad daylight, and kept a lamp burning at night. Her divorced daughter, Katie, who had returned home to live after her marriage breakup, shared her fear. Both lived in mortal dread of a sudden appearance of young Willett.

Several neighbors gathered at the house for a cottage prayer meeting on that never-to-be-forgotten afternoon. The Clarks and their daughter were converts—actually reconverts—to the Brashears kind of religion. Aunt Maggie had early "got the Holy Ghost," but the rest of the family remained as seekers. The express purpose of the meeting was to seek the coming of the Holy Ghost upon others of the family and anyone else who might desire such an experience.

At the appointed time, the neighbors and family took seats in the large dining room (the largest room in the house and just right for a gathering place). Katie, who had a small folding organ, sat down at it to play music for the hymn singing, which preceded prayer time.

Levi Clark, Evan and Maggie's grandson, lived with his family in the old servants quarters that stood just outside the backyard fence. Much given to playing pranks on people, the fun-loving boy knew that the prayer meeting in his grandparents' home was to seek the coming of the Holy Ghost. That, coupled with his knowledge of his grandmother's and Katie's fear of hants—especially an appearance of the deceased Willett—gave Levi a big idea. His plan was further encouraged when he noticed that his grandmother and Katie had put out a big washing of sheets that morning. Those white sheets gently swaying in the breezes that often swept down from Grandfather Mountain presented an almost irresistible urge to make good use of one of them.

With great anticipation, Levi waited until he heard the loud and lively singing, accompanied by that little organ and much hand clapping, rolling forth from the open dining room windows. Then he sprinted across the backyard, stripped a sheet from the line, and quietly slipped into the kitchen. He wrapped up in the sheet and eased into the windowless hall that led from the kitchen to the dining room. That hall stayed shadowy dark even on the brightest days, making an ideal grand entry point for an unexpected ghost.

The first hymn ended, and Katie announced the next hymn and placed her hands on the keys to begin. In the near silence as the crowd turned to the indicated number, an unearthly wail came from the hall as a white-sheeted figure suddenly appeared in the doorway. Then a moaning, quavering voice called out, "I'm a hant, I'm a hant. I'm Willett come back from the dead."

Needless to say, no one continued to look for the announced hymn! Some froze in horror; others screamed as they made for the nearest exit. One woman screeched out, "Lord, have mercy, we've done sung up the dead!"

Aunt Maggie, who'd been sitting by the hall door when the spectral figure appeared and claimed to be the ghost of Willett, looked straight at him and then called back, "Ye aire, ye aire! Great Gawd a'mighty, ye really aire!" Then she fell back in a faint and knew no more.

Katie screamed out, "Help us, Jesus!" then sprang up swinging around left and right as if deciding the better direction to run. In jumping up, her knees had thrown the organ over backward. She fell over it when she finally started to run that way, and went down in the floor on all fours, loudly breaking wind as she fell. She was up in a moment and went tearing out through the front hall, putting out more than wind, as she fled in panicky terror.

Her fright greatly intensified when she looked back and saw that the ghost had singled her out and was right behind her. She sailed through the front door, screaming to high heaven. Alas, the porch was rather narrow, and the steps did not line up with the door. Continuing to look behind her, she slammed into the porch railing, somersaulted over it, and landed in a rose bush, still profusely putting out evidence of her fear as she did so.

The ghost, apparently satisfied that he had done enough, jumped over the front steps, sprinted across the front yard, and disappeared into the nearby woods.

Indeed, a ghost had appeared at the prayer meeting, but the ghost wasn't holy!

PRAYER MEETING SURPRISE

The Timmons family lived way back in the piney woods of Ware County, Georgia. Ordinarily their home stayed as quiet as the backside of a country graveyard, but one sultry August afternoon, it was working alive with visitors. You see, a big holiness revival was going on at the nearby Lone Star schoolhouse, and each day the ladies of the community held a cottage prayer meeting. And on that particular day they met with Mrs. Timmons.

There must have been 20 or so in attendance—several old ladies sitting and fanning, a few innocent teenage girls recently saved and sanctified, and some in-betweens. Mr. Timmons had excused himself from the all-female gathering and had taken his Bible and sat down to read on the back porch. The ladies chose a long side porch and open hall for their place of prayer.

The couple's nitwit son, Hugh, craved attention and sometimes chose bizarre ways to obtain it. To keep the big, overgrown 18-year-old from distracting the meeting, his parents had told him to hoe the garden while the prayer meeting was in progress. He deeply resented this but made some semblance of obeying, at least until he heard singing from the side porch. For a few minutes he slowly hoed on, then stopped and leaned on the hoe handle listening. And a plan to become the center of attention slowly formed in his warped mind.

On the porch the girls finished a rousing hymn and allowed a testimony or two before beginning another. Some of the older ladies had begun to get in the pre-shouting mood, while the newly sanctified girls engaged in the holy dance. Then there was a brief silence before a new hymn began.

Suddenly from the far end of the hall came a wild, quavering whoop. Hugh sprinted down the hall and into the midst of the startled and shocked ladies, and he was naked as the day he was born! He'd sought attention and he'd sure found it. As if that were not shock enough, he circled around and through the gasping, swooning, and shrieking women, shouting a list of "ugly" words, four letter and otherwise. Wrapping his arms around one especially sanctified old-maid sister, and with his "main nakedness" right in her face (she was sitting), he called out, "Let's head fer the pine woods, Miss Anna Lou!"

But he released her as quickly as he had seized her. As she fell fainting to the floor, he grabbed one of the teenage girls and danced her around and around. He then jumped up on the porch rail and loudly crowed like a barnyard rooster.

By then his mother had come out of her shock. She lunged for him and called out, "Lard, have mercy. Hugh Timmons, take to the brush, quick!" All around her, ladies old and young were "just dying off," as they say in south Georgia. Some hid their faces, but many stared in apparent amusement or curiosity.

Mr. Timmons heard the commotion and darted through the kitchen to the side porch and his wife.

"Get him, get him quick," Mrs. Timmons yelled to her husband. "Get him and whup him good."

Mr. Timmons jumped down the steps and tore after Hugh. "I'll get him," he yelled back. Then the supposedly super-religious old man capped the stack by adding, "And when I get him, I'll whup the damned hell out of him."

WRONG REMEDY

The Adkins family, considered the "best livers" on Brushy Fork, owned the grandest farm and finest home in Breathitt County, Kentucky, and for that reason those who taught at the local one-room school usually boarded with them. In the summer of 1956, the charming schoolmarm was Miss Opal Whitt, a flaming redhead in her early 20s. She lived not too far away in Jackson, the county seat, but there were few good roads in the region at the time, so she chose to board rather than commute.

The Adkinses were fond of her, as were most of the residents of Brushy. Indeed, Mrs. Adkins had hopes that one of her five grown sons might someday "rope her in" as a bride, for not only did Miss Opal have every indication of being a capable teacher, but she seemed to enjoy homemaking, and she loved children.

She also faithfully attended the local Pilgrim Baptist Church, a fact that set well with the super-religious Adkins family. Miss Opal helped out with a Sunday school class that included 19-year-old Norman Adkins, the youngest of the five sons. If Miss Opal had any designs on an Adkins male, it seemed to be him, though he was about three years her junior.

But Miss Opal had a physical malady—plain old hemorrhoids, called the "piles" by the mountain folk. As is usually the case, her condition was intermittent but sometimes became so severe that it became difficult for her to walk or sit, except by edging out on a chair. Of course, such ailments were not discussed or even named in polite company, and many a student wondered why she walked or sat in such a strange manner.

Mrs. Adkins's aged mother—Granny Fields they called her—lived with her daughter and was an herb doctor of sorts. Though nearly blind, she still often sent a grandchild into the nearby woods to gather roots, bark, and leaves for her medicinal purposes.

When the suffering teacher finally consulted Granny Fields, the old woman calmly gave assurance of healing to her new patient: "Land, honey, I've cured many a case worser than yourn. They's a remedy in nature fer ever' condition—the good Lord sees to that—and I know jist what to get."

Within minutes, one of the young Adkins daughters was heading toward Fern Hollow with a detailed description of what to find. When she returned, Granny Fields had a pan of hot water ready for the healing plant. "It needs to be about like heavy gravy," she explained as she stirred vigorously and boiled the concoction down to a thick liquid.

Late that afternoon, Granny Fields ladled out her prescription. Handing the teacher a big cup full, she instructed, "Now, apply a lot of it directly to yore troubles, and ye ort to be well in a couple of days."

The Pilgrim Baptist Church planned to hold its weekly cottage prayer meeting with the Adkinses that night, so Miss Opal decided to take her bath and then apply the miracle medicine before everyone arrived. Just after supper, she dragged the washtub into her room, laid out her best green dress, and proceeded with her careful cleansing.

Meanwhile, folks from up and down Brushy began to assemble in the living room. Among them came brother Sol Thompson, who served as both the preacher and song leader of the local congregation. He brought a box of songbooks and his ever-present tuning fork.

Now, virtually everyone on Brushy always came to prayer meeting, from the oldest down to tiny tots. Of course, scattered among the crowd sat all five Adkins sons, combed and dressed for the much-loved midweek event. Norman, who had boasted a bit that he thought Miss Opal was leaning toward him, was looking forward to the grand entry of the object of his affections.

What an entry it turned out to be; neither he nor his neighbors would ever forget. As Sol began to pass out songbooks, Mr. Adkins called to his youngest son to fetch a bucket of fresh water, adding, "It's mighty hot, and folks are apt to get dry."

The lad, fearful that the errand might cause him to miss the appearance of Miss Opal, hastened to perform his father's request. In the meantime, inside the guest bedroom, the teacher had bathed long and carefully. Then while still completely nude, she swabbed on a generous amount of Granny Fields's pile reliever.

Now, it just happens that the miracle weed is similar to another low-growing plant. The granddaughter had been careful to follow instructions but not careful enough. And poor Granny could not see so well. While the miracle weed is indeed soothing, the other might be better termed as "fireweed," and fire it was. A superheated coal of fire would have been but little different than that generous slab of "balm."

To Miss Opal it felt exactly like a live coal had lodged in the most likely place. She lunged wildly left and right in sheer panic. At such moments, all else is forgotten; there must be relief. Nothing else matters; nothing else can be thought of. Her thought was water. Water, she must have water, and now!

The naked woman burst through the door and leaped forward among the startled and horrified crowd. She twisted in a most lewd manner, and her arms swung wildly, as her bare breasts rolled. All the while she was moaning, "Hot, hot! Oh, somebody help me cool it." No present-day, X-rated nudity show could have been more suggestive.

The effect on that crowd can hardly be described. A woman or two fainted. Others screeched out and jumped up trying to find something to wrap around the writhing woman. A few men hid their faces, but most of them did the expected: they leaned forward and looked intently at her, seemingly with extreme interest. Preacher Thompson bawled out, "Gawd a'mighty, Jesus, help this brazen huzzy. She's liable to tempt the brethren!"

Just about the time Miss Opal reached the center of the room, Norman arrived at the door with the bucket of cold well water. She saw it and sprang toward him. "Norman, Norman," she begged, "you've got what I need. Give it to me, give it to me quick." She swung around in front of him, bent over, and turned her burning south side. "Put it there quick," she yelled. "Give me all you've got."

Norman dropped the bucket and groaned, "Gosh, oh gooossh."

She felt the cold water around her feet and knew it was lost. Then she lunged over Norman—who by then had fallen to the floor—and ran to a nearby branch, where she sat down in the cooling waters.

The crowd muttered and paled in disbelief. "Lawsy, that must've been heifer weed," Granny Fields squeaked out, referring to a plant sometimes used by local farmers to bring heifers in heat. "I knowed it would work well on cattle but didn't reckon it would have sich a strong effect on young gals. Lydia Lou, go throw the rest out but quick, afore it makes a fool outta somebody else."

Needless to say, that night was still young when the schoolteacher packed and left Brushy Fork in disgrace. Norman Adkins seemed anxious to drive her home, but his mother would not hear of it. Instead, she and Mr. Adkins made the journey to Jackson with Miss Opal.

For years, even to the time of its consolidation with a larger school, Brushy Fork always employed an older male teacher.

WHERE TO HUNT

A large, imposing brick church still stands on a prominent corner in Chattanooga, Tennessee. Its membership, made up of a mostly elite segment of the local population, was more so at the time this incident took place in the late 1920s. The service was very ritualistic—and remains so, though to a lesser degree—and its patrician pastor fit in perfectly. Indeed, he loathed deviating the least degree from that ritual, so he detested having to give a mundane announcement once in a while.

Attending that church was a leading family named Hunt, including Miss Helen, who held a prominent position in a local bank. Her influence and status in the church were great, and her yearly pledge gave the budget a considerable boost. One Sunday Miss Helen reported to the pastor that she had found an expensive diamond ring in the church aisle, and asked him to make a statement about it from the pulpit. She thus hoped the rightful owner might appear. The pastor resented doing such a thing, but he knew he must not offend a Hunt, especially Miss Helen.

That morning he grudgingly found a slot in the ritual for the dreaded announcement. His words were few, but they were long remembered: "If anyone has lost a diamond ring go to Helen Hunt."

You guessed it! To the congregation, it sounded as if he had said "go to hell and hunt."

Unfortunately, I have no way of verifying that the Chattanooga incident actually occurred. The person who long ago gave me this story stated it as fact, though similar tales have been told by others, including Red Skelton, who used it as a joke.

THE WORLDLY LITTLE SAINT

The Holts were mountain missionaries who labored in the coalfields of southeastern Kentucky. They had moved to Perry County from upper Ohio to represent a super-sanctified holiness denomination. Their doctrines were somewhat difficult for the local folks to comprehend. Nevertheless, these sincere and earnest workers had gained a considerable following and had built a chapel on their creek.

Now, the Holts had three lovely children. The oldest, Danny, about ten years old, time and again had been admonished against the very suggestion of impure language. His parents also told him that holy saints should not so much as think of or mention certain sins, the worst among them being adultery and fornication. And on occasion his parents and others pointed him out to the numerous other children of the creek as a notable example of clean speech and conduct.

During the Easter revival, Rev. Fanning, an evangelist also from Ohio and, like the Holts, strong on pure and sinless living, preached those doctrines nightly. Near the end of the revival, the Holts honored the preacher with a covered dish supper at their quarters. As the ladies worked in the kitchen, the men and children gathered in the dining room, where the youngsters had to keep quiet while their elders talked of the day's lesson on setting affections on things above. When the supper was spread, Mrs. Holt, perhaps desiring to impress the guests with the piety of her darling Danny, asked him to give "that singing blessing that we've been teaching in Sunday school."

Little Danny's mind went blank; he could not remember a word of the singing blessing. Perhaps a bit stressed by a dining room full of sanctified saints, he was near panic.

The poor boy had been dwelling among youngsters of unclean lips, and from his subconscious there swelled up a little ditty that some of his older classmates had been singing behind the schoolhouse. So without a second thought, he "automatically" sang out:

> I'm a wildcat's kitten on my grandma's side,
> And I'm on the prowl tonight.
> And there'll be sore tailed pussycats all over creation
> After I make my rounds tonight.
> Look out, pussycats!

And as did his classmates, he scratched his foot backward at the last word and added "Meow, yow, wow wowwww."

For a long moment there was stunned silence. The next sound was a screech from Mrs. Holt, and then a "Lord, have mercy, Jesus," as she lunged toward her son.

And Danny lunged into the lap of the evangelist, seated at the child's side. There he loudly and hurriedly called out his defense: "But Brother Fanning likes it. He taught it to me a while ago." A lie had now followed "profanity."

You may be assured that there was a red-faced evangelist and a red-bottomed Danny for the rest of the evening.

If Conditions Are Right

The severe dry spell on Sand Mountain in northern Alabama had lasted so long that Rev. Rankin, the local Baptist preacher, convened a special prayer meeting. After calling the dusty crowd to order, the old brother made a plea for everyone to earnestly implore the Lord to make mud of the parched earth.

In no time he had his followers on their knees, loudly and in chorus praying for an end to the drought. But above the roar of those entreaties, the voice of the preacher became louder and louder, asking for the wind to blow from the east for three days.

When the supplications ended, a bold sister flatly asked Rankin why he was praying for a three-day east wind when all the rest were pleading for rain.

"Well, sister," he replied. "Ye can pray fer rain ever so long, and ye may er may not git it. But iffen the wind blows three days outen the east, all hell can't keep it from raining."

COUSIN TULL THROWS HIS VOICE

Some people said my grandfather's first cousin Tull Phillips had a million-dollar mind but never used it to financial advantage. One of his talents—or perhaps I should say his accomplishments—was ventriloquism. And though he likely never made much money by "throwing his voice," as hill-country folks called it, at times he did use it to some benefit.

While living in the Ozark Mountains of northern Arkansas, he knew "Uncle" Sam Alden, a traveling preacher who used a broken-down mule as his means of transportation. A rather large man, the preacher frequently took his obese (and that's putting it mildly) wife along with him. When both of them sat astride the decrepit mule, it appeared that the already swayback animal would surely collapse under its heavy burden. Sometimes their trips extended over several miles of rough mountain terrain, almost completely exhausting the poor beast.

Tender-hearted Cousin Tull got to feeling sorry for the worn-out, overburdened mule, and his cunning mind developed a plan to do something about the situation. He learned one day that Uncle Sam was to preach at the Bluff Springs schoolhouse, perhaps two miles from where Cousin Tull lived. He knew the road the preacher and his wife would travel, so he climbed a big oak tree that leaned out over the road about midway up a steep incline. Concealing himself in the dense, leafy branches, he waited. After a while, he heard the sound of slow, weary hoofbeats, along with the singing of Uncle Sam, who often belted out hymns as he rode along.

When the mule and his burden were directly under the oak, Tull masterfully used his art. In a coarse and loud voice, such as might befit a mule, he called out, "Why don't you two get off and walk up this hill? I'm just about wore out and can't go much farther."

Well, that poor beast didn't have his load for long. When the impact of what seemed to have happened soaked in, Uncle Sam stiffened and squalled, "Lord, have mercy!"

At the same instant, his wife screamed out, "This here mule's a-talkin'!" Then she slid backward, right over the mule's tail, and hit the road running toward home, soon disappearing around the bend at the foot of the hill.

Uncle Sam dropped the reins like they were red hot and sailed off so fast and far that he fell over the high bank at the roadside and tumbled down the hill toward a creek. He managed to jump to his feet before he got to it, but he wasn't ready to stop. Splitting the knee-deep creek wide open like it wasn't there, he disappeared into a cornfield on the other side. Cousin Tull long told that he could hear Uncle Sam yelling and the cornstalks snapping as the greatly frightened preacher tore across the field toward the woods beyond.

Tull didn't know what happened to the abandoned mule. But he did recall that Uncle Sam Alden and his wife always walked to the preaching places after their bout with the talking mule.

As one of those people who always look for the ideal place to put down roots but who never seem to find it, Tull traveled about a great deal, staying here and there for a time and then moving on. For about a year, he lived on a farm near Tatum, Texas, with a family named Stennis.

The family had two or three near-grown sons, and one Christmas Eve night on January 5th (many old-timers regarded January 6th as the true Christmas), a couple of neighbor boys came to spend the night. They had heard stories about supernatural goings-on at midnight on Christmas Eve, told to them by older members of the families. The boys knew Tull seemed to know about everything, so they asked him about the matter.

He answered that his mother, Mary Barthenia Houston Phillips, had often said that no matter how cold on that night, bees would swarm in the hives, certain plants would suddenly sprout leaves and stay green until dawning, and cows would get down on their knees and moan and groan as if praying.

The boys asked if Tull ever knew this to happen, and he immediately thought of a way to have a little fun. "Oh, yes," he replied. "I have seen and heard such things many times back in the hills of Arkansas." As the plan grew in his ever-alert mind, he said, "I tell you what, boys, there are no bees on this place, and I don't remember what plants are supposed to turn green. But there are cows out yonder in the barn, so we'll go out there just before midnight, and you will hear something you'll never forget."

The boys seemed eager for the experience, so before midnight they walked with him across the pasture to where the big barn stood, looking shadowy and mysterious in the dim moonlight. Several cows were apparently asleep in the stalls. Perhaps a few, including the herd bull, milled about back of the barn. Tull took a good position for voice-throwing and waited. Shortly there came a deep moan or two from the darkened stalls, then long groans and other weird sounds.

"They're about to start!" one of the boys nervously called out. "Let's get closer and listen. After all, we've never been to a cow prayer meeting before."

Cousin Tull saw his grand opportunity. Trying his best to make his unearthly voice sound like it came from the darkened stable, he said, "Lord, we want to offer our devotions to you, but there's some boys out there making fun of us. Now, send that big bull back there around here to give 'em a hard ride on his horns, so we can go on with our prayers."

Then Tull dropped his voice back to himself and excitedly called out, "Run, boys! Run for your lives, for I hear that bull a-comin'."

The boys didn't wait to see if they could hear the same thing. They shot across the pasture and jumped the fence in nothing flat. If the cows continued their midnight prayer meeting, they did it without an audience!

From Tatum, Cousin Tull drifted southward, finally reaching the Rio Grande Valley. Not long after arriving in in the beautiful city of Harlingen, he decided to attend services in a little Baptist church near where he boarded. He was shocked and surprised to find the church pastored by a minister he knew had been "run out" of northern Arkansas a few years before.

The preacher could not desist from having affairs with any woman who was willing. In Arkansas, he had been discovered in bed with a deacon's wife. Consequently, he abandoned his family and left in quite a hurry, never telling folks there where he went. Tull had now discovered him 900 miles away in Cameron County, Texas, where the minister claimed to be a widower.

Tull soon learned that apparently the leopard had not changed his spots. Even though the preacher had led the Texas church for only a few months, a scandal was already brewing. One of the prominent members had a 17-year-old daughter, Gladys, who had married a much older man a year or so before. But her husband had gone away on a construction job and would not return for several months. Rumors were circulating that Gladys was showing signs of being mighty fond of the new minister, who evidently didn't mind her attention in the least.

Gladys lived with her husband's widowed grandmother, and back of the house was a fairly large orange grove. One Sunday night at the close of the service, someone saw Gladys slip a note into the preacher's hand as he stood at the door greeting the departing congregation. Her action really started tongues wagging.

Tull heard, and using a little logic and much leftover information from his wild youthful days, he reasoned out what proved to be a correct appraisal of what might happen. On Monday night, hiding in some tall, dense shrubbery that separated the backyard of the grandmother's house from the orange grove, he waited patiently.

About midnight, a tall figure slipped into the orange grove and stood in the shadows, peering toward the darkened house. Before long, Gladys emerged quietly from the back door, carrying a quilt under her arm. She hastened across the yard and passed through the shrubbery very close to where Cousin Tull had secreted himself.

Suffice it to say that before he slipped from the shrubbery shortly before dawn, he well knew that indeed the leopard had not changed his spots. Anyone in need of pastoral services that night would not have found the minister at the parsonage.

Though Tull said nothing about his discoveries to anyone, gossip did increase that week about the suspicious situation, so much so that the pastor felt compelled to make a defensive statement at the next Sunday's service. Tull sat on the front pew, within a few feet of the pulpit, in order to make what he planned to do a little easier. Gladys sat on the other front pew, all moon-eyed for her new lover.

After the song service ended—and there wasn't much spirit in it—the pastor arose in self-righteous dignity and looked out over the assembly. "There's been a lot of loose talk this week," he began, "about me and one of the dear young sisters of this congregation. Now, I can explain everything. I'm going to tell you the truth about the matter, and you'll see how wrong you have been. But before I get into that, I think we all ought to bow our heads and have silent prayer, so our bad feelings can get sanctified, and get prepared to forgive and forget."

As the time of supposed quiet prayer began, Cousin Tull saw the opportunity he had been waiting for. He "threw" his voice right into the mouth of the deceitful pastor, or so it seemed: "Well, folks, I think I will just tell you the truth. Why, sure, me and Gladys have been meeting up there in that orange grove behind the house where she's staying, and we've sure done the devil's wrestle several times. And we're going to keep on doing it every time we get the chance. I don't care what you bunch of numbskulls think or do. I'm going to have Gladys in spite of hell or high water!"

During the wave of stunned gasps that swept over the congregation, Gladys jumped up and, waving her finger at the startled pastor, screeched out, "Why, you lying devil! You told me that if I'd play marriage with you, you wouldn't tell nobody. Now I've done it, and you done told it on us."

Her outburst left no doubt in the minds of the parishioners. And it certainly left no doubt in the mind of a brother of Gladys's husband. He leaped up and, with pocketknife in hand, made for the greatly puzzled minister, who was waving his arms about and trying to be heard over the uproar, desperately trying to explain that he hadn't said anything. When he saw the enraged man coming at him with the open knife, he whirled, leaped out the back door, and fled. The last time anyone saw him in that area, he was half running and half jumping through a field of okra behind the church. He gave no official resignation, but needless to say, that little Baptist church was without a pastor.

Harlingen, Texas, became the end of the line for roving Cousin Tull Phillips. He died there in 1936 and is buried in the town cemetery. I spent a few days in Harlingen several years afterward, and I searched through that cemetery but could not locate his grave.

Here I will add a note that may be of interest to those who like to know of the strange or unusual. When Cousin Tull lived in Johnson County, Arkansas, he carved his picture on a beechnut tree that stood on the Sam Phillips farm about five miles down Piney Creek below Fort Douglas post office. (I was born and reared on an adjoining farm.) In the summer of 1936, folks passing by noticed that the tree, so recently green and flourishing, had suddenly withered away and died. Within a short time came word of Tull's death 900 miles away. The superstitious folks in the neighborhood thought this "meant something," and they talked of it for years.

THE STRANGE BAPTISM OF REV. CAIN BROWN

Rev. Cain Brown, a dyed-in-the-wool Hard-Shell Baptist, often declared that all who were not baptized by immersion were heretics. Little did he know that one day he would be baptized by pouring. He preached once a month at the Big Butterfly Baptist Church in Perry County, Kentucky, and the congregation bragged that there wouldn't be any better preaching "nowhere in Perry County."

The minister lived far down the Kentucky River at Chavies, so he rode the train to the Big Butterfly depot on Friday and walked the remaining three miles up the creek, where he stayed in one of the local homes until Monday. On the occasion of his unexpected baptism by pouring, he had stopped at Sim Rye's place for his weekend lodging. The Rye family, somewhat better off than most of the folk on upper Big Butterfly, owned a huge two-pen log house with a full story above and a large detached kitchen in the backyard. And they always had plenty of corn bread and turnip greens on their table, along with buttermilk, sweet potatoes, boiled meat, and honey.

After a fine supper, the Ryes and their guest enjoyed a watermelon before turning in for the night. As was common in the community then, visitors usually had to share a room, and frequently a bed, with members of the family. But at the Rye home, Rev. Brown had a big plump feather bed to himself, even though it was located in the same room with Mr. and Mrs. Rye and Mrs. Rye's father. Since the room was dark, the preacher could stretch out on top of the sheets and enjoy the cool breezes wafting up from the spring branch that flowed just beyond the yard. He knew he would wake up before daylight to cover himself and thus protect his modesty. In minutes, he was sound asleep, lying on his back and loudly snoring, his mouth open wide.

Mr. and Mrs. Rye's four grown sons slept in a room directly above where their parents and the minister slept. Now, those were the days long before Perry County had the least semblance of indoor plumbing. Consequently, the family kept a chamber pot in every bedroom, both as a convenience and a safety feature. It saved one from cold in winter and the danger of snakes in summer. The big, metal chamber pot in the boys' room often filled to near overflowing before someone carried it down the back stairs and emptied it.

Not long after retiring, one of the boys felt a need for the chamber pot. He arose and groped in the dark, searching for it. After a step or two, he doubled a big toe against the bedpost. In pain and anger, cursing under his breath, he started swinging the injured foot back and forth. And wouldn't you just know it, the third swing centered the near-full chamber pot.

Over it went, the lid rolling and the contents swooshing out. Unfortunately, when the Rye home was built, uncured flooring had been used upstairs, resulting in half-inch cracks all over the place. And down through one of those cracks, directly over the guest bed, rushed a waterfall of liquid. The torrent hit Rev. Brown about mid-body and quickly spread upward until he caught a big gush right in his open mouth. He sprang up, crashed

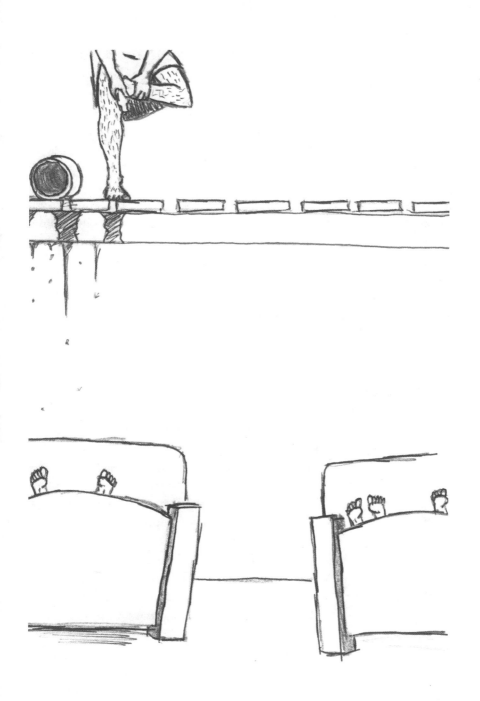

into the wall, and fell back across the bed in time to get another sheet of liquid across his chest. Then he somersaulted into the aisle between the beds, coughing and sputtering.

The Ryes awoke in astonishment, just as Rev. Brown fell across the foot of their bed, spitting and vomiting violently. But in a moment, he was up and dashing for the door into the dogtrot (open hall). Through it he went into the backyard. It was a bad move, for he startled the old hound dog, who seized his shirttail and tore it from him. Then the dog grabbed him in the most likely place. The preacher lunged for the porch and bedroom door, with the hound dog hanging on behind. Slinging the animal loose, he dashed wildly into the room.

"Whar's my infernal britches?" he roared as he felt wildly about. "I've done been baptized with stuff out of a chamber pot and bit by that damned hound dog till I can't set down fer a month. I'm gettin' outta here rat now!"

Rev. Brown found his pants and in no time was hightailing it down Big Butterfly. The minister had been baptized by pouring, but it wasn't holy water!

EXCITING SERVICE

Those who crave excitement in church services would not have been disappointed had they been in attendance at the Bristol Baptist Church (now known as First Baptist Church) in Bristol, Virginia, on Sunday, May 13, 1877. The church was located on the same lot as now, but the building in use at that time faced Main (now State) Street, whereas it now faces Virginia Street. As now, it was then a vital force in the religious life of the community, well attended and heavily supported by its faithful members.

In those days, that church kept close watch on the personal lives and actions of its parishioners. The slightest infraction of the church rules could bring about a church trial and possible exclusion from membership. And certainly the church required that its members not only be holy but to always talk holy, apparently operating on the premise that what is truly in a person will "come out through the mouth." Those who wanted to remain in the membership had to constantly guard their tongues.

Most were successful in this endeavor, but under extreme pressure or excitement, words occasionally slipped out that, if heard by other members of the church, or even outsiders, might cause swift dismissal of the offending member. Of course, such an offense would seldom occur in the church building, where virtually everyone made a supreme effort to be on good behavior. But once it did!

That particular Sunday was a bright, balmy day, perhaps partially the cause of an extra large crowd attending the morning service. Among them was Alden Hinchey, a member from almost the beginning of the church. He had once served as an officer in the church and was well-known for his Christian testimony and generous giving both to the church and to other worthy causes. And his fellow church members loved to hear him pray. It seems that he was especially gifted in this respect.

When it came to prayer time during that long-ago service, Brother Hinchey was called upon. He stood and began what his fellow worshipers expected to be a long and fervent entreaty. He always sat next to the aisle on the fifth pew back, and whenever he stood to pray, he would gradually work his way out into the aisle. Sometimes, if he really "got in the spirit," he might walk up and down the aisle a bit. That morning he had made it to the aisle and was getting with it, swinging his arms about and slapping his side and thigh as he became more and more carried away in the spirit.

Suddenly the sanctuary resounded to the loud report of a pistol shot. As the congregation jumped and stiffened, old Brother Hinchey also jumped sky high, then began dancing around, holding up one foot. And as editor Fowler of the *Bristol News* reported it, "He began to shout words that were somewhat less than holy." Less than holy indeed! He actually cussed a blue streak as he jumped and danced about.

A pistol he was carrying in his pocket—virtually all Bristol men went armed in those days—had discharged and shot him through the right foot. It was a sad day for Brother Hinchey. He not only shot himself through the foot, he was also dismissed from the church membership. Though he was well-loved and respected by virtually everyone in the church, rules were rules and must be followed.

There was no need for a trial. All present had witnessed his transgression. The only member not voting was John R. Dickey, who had gone running for Dr. H. T. Berry as soon as he saw what had happened.

Baptist justice was fast in those days. Alden Hinchey had been voted out of the church before the good doctor arrived!

THE SAGA OF TICKLING TOM GAYHEART

Folks all over Walker County, Georgia, said that Tom Gayheart was "quare." And I suppose he was, for only someone a little off in the head would do what he was always doing. His strange mental condition came about, everyone said, because his unmarried mother and father were first cousins and were both drunk when she became pregnant. He made his home with his grandfather, who lived in the most remote part of the county in a rough hollow. But Tom wasn't happy there, so he wandered about, staying a while with anyone who would keep him.

His great delight was to poke people in some sensitive spot, especially those he knew were "goosey." Some people when goosed would jump and holler; some would call out what they were thinking; others would say whatever had been whispered to them just before goosing. Tom especially liked to goose people in church, for they often would call out something a little less than holy.

One time near High Point, he found Sid Bingham standing in the crowd that had gathered outside the community church for dinner on the ground. Sid was engrossed in conversation with a much younger, red-headed beauty. When Tom slipped up behind him and goosed him in the lower ribs, Sid jumped, looked straight at the lady, and yelled out, "Honey, I'd sure like to take you to the brush."

Sid's reaction created quite a stir in the crowd and caused the young woman to bolt into the meetinghouse. Tom, shrieking with laughter, ran back down the trail, and Sid grabbed up a rock and took off after him. Alas, Sid, too fat to be fleet of foot, couldn't get close enough to do him any damage.

In the same community stood a one-room schoolhouse. Sally Temple, a super-religious spinster, presided over the classes and devoted an hour every day teaching the Bible to the entire school. One hot day as she sat in a window and taught, Tom slipped up and goosed her.

She threw the Bible on the floor and jumped across the room, shouting out her thoughts: "Most of you dumb devils will never learn God's Word. I'm wasting my breath." Then realizing what she had said, the old maid ran into the schoolyard looking for Tickling Tom.

She had no difficulty finding him. He was rolling in the dirt, nearly hysterical with fits of laughter. His laughter soon changed, however, for that gentle Christian woman leaped upon him like an angry wildcat and gave him the beating of his life.

But the punishment didn't cure Tickling Tom. A few days later, he found "Long" Frank Felkins plowing a field a few miles south of the schoolhouse. He knew that Frank, a deacon in the local Baptist church, was a kind and easy-going Christian gentleman who had boasted that on those rare occasions when he became angry, he quickly prayed about it and cleansed his soul of the sin. "I never let the sun go down upon my wrath," Frank often declared.

Before the unsuspecting farmer knew anyone was near, Tom goosed him real strong. In a fit of rage, Long Frank jumped straight up and "cut such a shine" that his horse ran away with the plow, charging all over the field and destroying several rows of young corn. Tom had already fallen down in the freshly plowed ground with his usual laughing fit. His victim quickly yanked off his leather belt and proceeded to horse whip the prankster with the buckle end, even running behind him and still lashing as Tom made for the nearby bushes. And I suspect that many suns set upon his wrath before he ever forgave Tickling Tom. Anytime or anywhere Frank saw him, an old-timer told me, he would "just make for him, ready to do battle."

I suppose Tickling Tom decided next to find safety in distance. He soon showed up in the lower end of the county near Center Post. As he walked into the community, he saw a funeral in progress at a small family cemetery. "Aunt" Lucy Yates had died, and preacher Dan Wilkins was conducting her graveside service.

Dan was one of the most respected and well-known preachers in southern Walker County. In his sermons he bore down on the necessity of using pure speech before an unbelieving world. But his stand on the matter was sorely tested that day by the antic of Tickling Tom Gayheart.

Tom eased into the crowd unnoticed by the mourners. When Dan began the committal prayer, Tom edged closer until he stood directly behind the minister. All heads were bowed, and most eyes were closed. Suddenly Tom reached out and goosed the preacher.

Dan turned out to be very goosey. He yelled out like a madman and landed with one wild leap right in the open grave. (The casket hadn't been suspended over it, as is the custom now.) Once in the hole, he hopped up and down a time or two, yelling at the top of his voice. Many in the crowd gasped at the unexpected development brought on by the roving prankster.

When the preacher finally came to his senses and realized what had happened, he leaned out over the top of the grave and peered angrily at Tom, who by then was on the ground, rolling among the gravestones and laughing like a maniac. Then Dan—the advocate of pure speech—

shocked the crowd by yelling out, "You low-down son-of-a-bitching devil. I'm gonna beat the damned hell out of you when this here funeral's over with."

But Dan didn't have a chance to carry out his threat. Tickling Tom sprang up like a scared deer and fled up the northbound road. He knew he better leave the community, but after about a mile, he had a chance to goose again. On a porch near the road he saw "Slim" Pete Wilkins, son of preacher Dan Wilkins, intently courting Miss Della Horne, as they sat in a swing.

Della was "powerful religious," as the neighbors sometimes described her. But I suppose because she and Slim Pete were so near to being married, she was not resisting his arming her up and placing long kisses on her lips. After all, almost everyone in the neighborhood was down at the cemetery, and no one would know.

But Tom knew, and he also knew that the pair was so absorbed in one another that he could easily slip up on them. Not even a creaking porch board got their attention. Without warning, Tom goosed Pete's lower ribs. The love-struck young man was just as goosey as—if not more than—his father.

And Della must have been in great shock when Slim Pete tore loose from their strong, long kiss and yelled out like he had been thunderstruck. In an instant he sprang up, and with his arm still around her, poor Della was flung forward and down. She hit the porch floor and rolled like a loose bottle right off the edge and into her mother's prize zinnia bed.

By that time, Tickling Tom was bounding like a deer across the yard. He jumped the fence and ran up the road, laughing at the top of his voice.

Slim Pete sprinted across the porch with the intent of catching and beating the tar out of his tormenter. However, when he leaped off the porch, one foot landed in a chamber pot that Mrs. Horne had set out so drippings from the roof might wash it out. Pete swung his foot wildly around, trying to rid himself of the jar. His foot soon hit the foundation stones of the porch, and the jar shattered, inflicting a severe cut or two on his lower leg and ankle. In a rage he hopped up and down, cussing a blue streak.

Heretofore, Pete had used his father's brand of pure language around his sweetheart. Alas, when she heard him, she broke their engagement, vowing to never marry a man who would cuss like that.

You know, that may have been a unique situation. From the beginning of civilization, do you suppose there has ever been another engagement called off because of a broken chamber pot?

Needless to say, Tickling Tom Gayheart left the Center Post community far behind that day. He wound up near Wildwood in adjoining Dade County, his only known foray outside of Walker County. "He was pert nigh in Tennessee," said my informant. And it was there that he was cured of his tickling mania.

In Dade County, Tickling Tom "took up," as the saying goes in that part of Georgia, with the Will Stidham family. The Stidhams owned a large but plain house way back in the woodsy part of the county. "Uncle" Will had reared two families—nine children each by both of his wives—and several of the last set still lived at home. He had also partly reared a niece, Miss Nedra Hasseltine. Though she had returned to her father's home in Trenton, she spent part of the summer with her greatly beloved Uncle Will's family.

Not long after Tickling Tom arrived, he was working one afternoon with the Stidham family in a field near their home. All of a sudden the air was rent by screams from Mrs. Stidham, who had been resting for a spell on the front porch after preparing and serving a "work hands style" (large) dinner for the midday meal. All dropped their hoes and ran to the house. There they learned that Mrs. Stidham had been quietly sitting in her worn but comfortable old rocker, when she was startled to see a giant rattlesnake slither out from under the floor and crawl across the yard, where it disappeared in a dense gooseberry patch. Some of them looked around a little, but no one wanted to do much searching in such a weedy place.

A few days later one of the younger Stidham children encountered the rattler in the family garden, but it crawled away before anyone could answer the child's call for help. Then one night, after the family had gone to bed, the dog raised an alarm out in the corner of the yard. Will Stidham quickly arose and went to see what was going on. In the moonlight he saw the rattlesnake crawl through the fence into the gooseberry patch. However, he wasn't about to search for a big, dangerous snake in the dark.

Needless to say, by then the Stidham family had a severe case of the rattlesnake jitters. They shunned weedy, brushy places and went out at night only when absolutely necessary.

A community prayer meeting had been set at the Stidhams for the next Friday night. As a precautionary measure, Will spread the word that all those who planned to come should watch for the big snake and stay within the clear path.

The day before the prayer meeting, Will's visiting niece, Nedra, became severely constipated. On Friday morning, while helping her aunt prepare breakfast, she mentioned her troublesome ailment. Mrs. Stidham knew just what to do, and by eleven o'clock that morning, she had a big pot of poke greens (called poke sallet in that region) cooking on the kitchen stove. Usually a "good bait" (large amount) of this potent southern herb will quickly cure the worst case of constipation. Nedra ate freely and even drank some of the juice in which it was cooked. Then she waited in hope.

As the crowd gathered that night, Tickling Tom heard Nedra tell some of the neighbor girls that she was expecting to have to go down behind the gooseberry patch before the end of the meeting. (The women and girls in the Stidham family used that location for bathroom purposes.) Nedra went on to ask two or three of the girls to go with her, so they could help watch out for the dreaded big rattler.

Tom quickly concluded that he might have a chance to do some real goosing. He slipped away from the crowd and hastened down past the gooseberry patch, where he found a couple of rocks set closely together. In spite of the snake scare, he lay down in the bushes and weeds, right behind the "squatting rocks" that he knew the ladies used for the obvious purpose. There he patiently waited, at times shaking with laughter at the thought of Nedra's reaction to his plan.

Back at the house, the prayer meeting had barely started when Nedra developed a feeling indicating that the poke sallet was about to work. Within moments she and the other girls hurried past the gooseberry patch. Once there she quickly arranged her clothes for the duty at hand and squatted above the two rocks.

Tickling Tom silently slid a bit forward, raised his hand directly below her, and did some quick tickling. Nedra, in a flash, envisioned the big rattler crawling under her and raising his head. She squalled out, hopped up, and staggered backward, screaming that the big rattler was right under her. Still in a semi-squatting position, she wound up over Tickling Tom's face. And whether by action of the poke sallet, or by extreme fear, her constipation was suddenly, explosively, and profusely relieved.

Beneath her, Tom had just thrown his mouth wide open to laugh, when his face was covered with the natural product of Nedra's constipation relief. He tried to jump up, which sent his nose right into the place where the first deluge came from, triggering another violent explosion. Now, what wasn't done to him the first time was done during the second torrent.

About that time the girl nearest Nedra screamed out, "Land, it ain't a snake; it's a big old man under you!"

Snake or man—it didn't matter. By then, Nedra had regained her balance and went jumping in long leaps toward the house, as the frightened girls followed behind her. They were not the only ones running. Tickling Tom was up and tearing down the hill toward the spring branch, spitting, coughing, gagging, and vomiting as he went.

He never returned to the house. Apparently he struck out for Walker County that night. A day or two later he showed up at his grandfather's house way back in the remote hollow where he was born and reared. Some say that he rarely left the area again. Apparently his bad experience with Nedra Hasseltine cured him of his compulsion to goose or tickle anyone, for if he had done such again, no one ever knew about it.

PRAYING FOR THE MILK GOAT

Nat Stickley was not one of the brightest members of the little Baptist church located a few miles west of Eubanks, in Pushmataha County, Oklahoma. But for years, he had attended faithfully, even though his hearing was so bad that he could hardly hear a word of the pastor's sermons. Rain or shine, come what may, he never missed.

He especially enjoyed the weekly prayer meetings, likely because he had a childlike faith, sincerely believing that the Almighty would grant even his most insignificant petition. Some of Nat's prayer requests bordered on the humorous, but the pastor always repeated them to the congregation as if they were important and urgent matters. One time, for instance, Nat asked for prayers that his milk didn't "turn" the next day, because he didn't see how he'd find time to churn until the following day. (No one knows what happened to the milk.)

He owned a small farm adjoining the church property. On it he kept a variety of farm animals, including a favorite milk goat named Mindy. Late one Wednesday afternoon, Nat discovered Mindy missing, as sometimes happened when she felt the need of consorting with a billy goat for a while. At such times she would break out of the pasture and roam the countryside in search of a billy friend.

In spite of his concern for the stray goat, Nat went on to prayer meeting. Before the service began, he asked the pastor to remember his missing goat in prayer, and the pastor kindly agreed to do so.

In addition to Nat's prayer request, the pastor had already received one for Sister Mandy, who was sick and in the hospital at McAllister, several miles away. When prayer time came, he asked the members to "Pray much for sister Mandy, who is away from us tonight. Pray for her speedy return to us."

Now, to Nat Stickley's greatly impaired ears, it sounded like the preacher was seeking prayers for Mindy's return. He brightened up. "Do pray for her," he said. "I think she's just off huntin' a billy, but I don't think she's needin' one, fer she's already givin' the most milk of the bunch!"

The poor pastor needed a long time to get that crowd thinking in a serious vein again!

Twisting the Quotes

When I was a young lad going to a one-room school in Fort Douglas, Arkansas, the teacher asked each student to read a Bible verse every morning before the studies of the day commenced. Mistakes were occasionally made, but none so memorable as the blooper made by my classmate Nolan Hughes, when he tried to read St. Matthew 23:24, which says, "Ye blind guides, which strain at a gnat, and swallow a camel." But Nolan made the text a little more difficult; he read it as "strain at a gate and swallow a sawmill."

Our 1944 Christmas program at that same school featured the carol "While Shepherds Watched Their Flocks by Night." One first grader went home and told his mother that the students sung a beautiful song that day. When the mother inquired which one, he replied, "While Shepherds Washed Their Socks by Night."

It is my belief that thousands of lies are told every Sunday morning at the doorways of churches all across the land when some parishioners shake the minister's hand and say they enjoyed his sermon. *Endured* would often be a more truthful word. Many times the person thus saying was bored and could hardly wait for the sermon to end. Here in East Tennessee a member shook his pastor's hand one day and told the truth. "Pastor," he said, "your sermon today was like the peace and mercy of God. It passed all understanding, and I thought it would endure forever."

Also in East Tennessee, a nervous young minister was preaching a trial sermon before a rather large church. He started to quote a verse of scripture, telling what he would do if elected pastor of that church. The verse is about visiting the sick, raising the dead (he didn't really mean to do that, but it is part of the verse), and casting out devils. He got it a little mixed up, though, and said that the Bible admonishes us to "cast out the sick, to heal the dead, and raise the devil!" But his story has a happy ending. In spite of his slipup, the congregation elected him as pastor, and he served that church faithfully and successfully for many years.

Finis

Though now at the end of this book, it is by no means the end of my collection of "holy grinning tales," and the collection is still growing. If the response to this book is great enough, I just might compile and publish more tales that I hope would not only cause you to grin, but would give you fits of side-splitting laughter. I also invite you to share your grinning tales with me. I may be reached at the address given in the opening pages of this book.